THE LIVING RU

APOLOGIA

MIEKE MOSMULLER

THE LIVING RUDOLF STEINER

APOLOGIA

OCCIDENT PUBLISHERS

Original title: Der lebendige Rudolf Steiner
Translated by Ruth Franssen
Proofreading by Terry Boardman

Occident Publishers
Postbox 306
5110 AH Baarle Nassau
The Netherlands
Telefon: 00-31-13-5077240 / E-mail: info@occident-publishers.com
Internet: www.occident-publishers.com

Graphic design: Martijn Franssen
ISBN / EAN: 978-90-75240-33-7

Copyright © 2013 Occident Publishers
All rights reserved

CONTENT

THIRD PART

FOURTH PART

Preface

I had already been thinking about writing 'the living Rudolf Steiner' for a long time. What originally stimulated me to write about Rudolf Steiner as a living spiritual being was the discussion paper by Ramon Brüll and Jens Heisterkamp on the issue of the allegations of racism against Rudolf Steiner and the underlining of this issue by many prominent anthroposophers. (2008).

Rudolf Steiner (1861-1925) died in 1925, so he is no longer alive. He wrote an autobiography (unfinished), in which he portrayed his spiritual-intellectual development for everyone to read. He described how this related to his environment and to the people who played a major or minor part in his life. Furthermore, there are several biographies in which Rudolf Steiner's work and life are extensively described. But writing another biography is not what I wanted to achieve with this book.

Rudolf Steiner has left us with a mighty oeuvre, his Collected Works, a 'Gesamtausgabe', which includes over 350 books. Of those just a few (28) were actually written by him; the majority are notes or printed versions of the shorthand transcripts of his lectures which he held for more than 20 years, as well as his articles in magazines, letters etc.

Also he 'left' behind an anthroposophical society. It is an international society, with a central executive at the headquarters of the society in Dornach (Switzerland). This society was refounded by Rudolf Steiner himself in 1923/24 (the ‚Christmas Conference‘), and it exists up to the present day. There are actually three sources to which one can refer when one wants to get to know Rudolf Steiner: the biographies (including the autobiography), the 'Gesamtausgabe' and the society.

But there is also a fourth source, out of which one can not create immediately, because it has to be *opened* first. Where the first three sources are open to everybody, the fourth is closed for everybody. And where the first three sources give only external information – although the *content* may not be external – for they are formed by the intellect and finally come from observing with the senses (reading, hearing, looking), the fourth source gives the possibility, to observe the inner being of Rudolf Steiner – in so far as it is permitted to a human being to do so.

The inner being of a man does not die with his body. It remains alive and develops itself further. This book is created from the fourth source and that accounts for its title: The *Living* Rudolf Steiner. This human being is still there, either in the spiritual world, or again incarnated in a physical body. He observes what is created from his three sources, his legacy and what comes from it.

I have not written this book only for anthroposophers, but for everyone who has an interest in spirituality and wants to get to know this Master of the Occident better. Therefore I have tried, in describing him, to hold to the (challenging) middle - on the one hand not giving too many details, and on the other hand, not thinking that everything is already known.

FIRST PART

The fourth source
A justification

How is the fourth source opened? It is opened by walking a certain path – the path of loving insight or understanding love. Even in daily life friends only open up to one when one's insight is 'lived'. However, when one has to get to know someone through his writings, it becomes seriously difficult. An insight must be developed that is no longer intellectual but also not only receptive.

One only finds this fourth source of insight 'beyond' pure thinking, 'beyond Saturn'; it must live beyond the stars.'[1] That should not be just a poetical expression, but must be a new path of knowledge. Pure thinking is a thinking that only thinks thoughts that do not originate from the senses. Daily thinking is only sometimes pure, because it almost only has sensual (sensorial) content. Aristotle's statement is well-known: *Nothing is in the intellect that was not first in the senses*. In our time we must add to this: *except for the intellect itself*. Thus one finds true pure thinking in the thinking of the intellect itself.

This fourth source of knowledge can be found through the indications given for nurturing spiritual insight that are presented by ... Rudolf Steiner.

He has given us the ways to prepare ourselves to get to know an individuality from the inside in his or her full livingness. When we have applied these methods, we develop in ourselves the ability to gain lively insight into the human being. Should we not also apply these methods to

---

[1]   See Friedrich Schiller: *Ode to Joy*

understand the individuality of the teacher himself?

The fourth source thus lies beyond pure thinking.

In pure thinking one has already had to leave behind all one's opinions and judgments, which are in the intellect. One has developed a thinking that has exerted itself so much in order to live only in thinking itself, that it has released itself from egoism, from subjective sympathy and antipathy. It is a thinking which thus can think along with *every* content, totally objectively, without opinion or judgment – because these cannot survive in pure thinking. One only *experiences* the content, and it is a pure experiencing, free of judgment. *Patience* in experiencing finally provides us with judgment: we do not form it, but it happens to us.

I myself started reading the books and lectures of Rudolf Steiner in 1983. In the year 1986 I began with systematic meditation and a meditative contemplation of *The Philosophy of Freedom*. In 1987 I had my first experience of pure thinking, together with pure Self-experience. Since then, I have been studying and meditating on the work of Rudolf Steiner with a capacity which 'lies beyond the stars'[2] . In 1994 I described this capacity in a book: 'Seek the Light that rises in the West'[3] and in 2005 in 'The Holy Grail'.[4]

With this ability which I have had now for over 20 years, I turn to the teacher, who still lives, who one can find, who one can recognize.

This book originates from no fanatical worship, but from

---

[2] See the lecture of 6 Feb. 1923 in Rudolf Steiner, *Anthroposophical Community Building*, GA 257

[3] Mieke Mosmuller, *Seek the Light that Rises in the West*, Occident 1994

[4] Mieke Mosmuller, *De heilige Graal* (The Holy Grail), Occident 2005

a pure notion, a pure understanding, which unfolds in relationship with the sense of the I.

Reading the works of Rudolf Steiner

Reading is a wonderful human skill. We can form words out of a combination of signs, and from a combination of words we can form sentences, which we understand. We add these comprehended contents to our already existing concepts, or else we find a contradiction or no connection at all.

When we can insert the new content in our thinking organism, we say, relieved: yes, that is clear!

If we find no connection, we say: I do not understand this. A healthy soul will search further until the connection is found and it can say to itself: now I have understood it! However, the 'unhealthy mind' will, when it does not understand, very soon declare: that is not right!

Most difficult is the inner experience of a contradiction. Hereby a complicated process gets going, and the reader must test himself. Is it subjective antipathy? Has something been said that is unpleasant? Has what was said offended against any pre-existing opinions or judgments? Or is it an objective antipathy? What should one do with the contradiction?

The unhealthy mind does not even test itself at all; it is impulsive and does not look at itself in its own soul. It quickly 'exclaims': I have a different opinion! I do not agree with that! That is not right at all! etc.
Being able to take up or having to reject the contents of spiritual science in the beginning strongly depends on the character that the soul has always had. Therefore, one

cannot convince people who strongly resist spiritual science. One can not know how it works in the depth of the
soul. Anthroposophy may be rejected as uncongenial by
superficial thinking and feeling habits, while in the depths
something totally different is going on. A free state of mind
in relation to spiritual science must be absolutely respec-
ted. One can truly only strive oneself to read with as little
prejudice as possible, and at most explain to other people
what is actually written there. Whether this is accepted or
rejected is a question of the other's freedom.

Let us assume that a human being willingly relates to
spiritual science, that he can take in its contents without
irritation, that he can understand on the whole what is of-
fered. How should such a person read?

Actually, all casual, swift reading should be avoided. It
is better to read only *one* line, and take it in the right way
than to read a whole chapter or a whole lecture quickly.
Not the desire to know must encourage the reader, but the
desire to increase one's insight into the content as well as
one's power and capacities. In fact, the whole work of Rudolf Steiner is intended to become something living, that
grasps life, as the leaves sprout on the branches in spring.
However, it can also remain wood, from which nothing
new can grow. It then stiffens even more, becomes only
material for quotation and in this is given over to dogmatism. Not a word of spiritual science should ever become
dogma, because that is as unknown to it as death is to life.
However, seeds of death exist everywhere in spiritual science where only the intellect is operative. Too much life can
also be present when the intellect withdraws altogether in
favour of feeling. The intellect *itself* must become alive, and
then the whole of spiritual science which has been taken in
will become alive and be able to keep growing, blossom,

flourish, bear fruit, germinate…

That can only be achieved when one learns to read from the fourth source. Then one takes in the words purely just as they are written there, the connections as purely as they are described. If one understands it, then one lets the concept stream deeply into the mind, into the heart, into the will – and one acknowledges indisputably: you have only understood a very small part. Your understanding can grow, increase, deepen, expand.

If one does *not* understand, the difference between this and understanding is only gradual. Then one lets the not-understanding stream deeply into one's mind and acknowledges: it becomes a question, and the answer will be given if one is patient.

It is like *breathing*: reading is breathing out, the deepening is breathing in… It is like nutrition: reading is like eating, the deepening is like digestion. Thus one must learn to *live* the text; as in the physical body life processes occur, one should similarly take in spiritual science *so* that life processes occur. The reader of spiritual science should imagine this most intensively and try to come to this imagination while reading over and over again.

Thus the reader should *warm* the lines himself, take them in warmly instead of indifferently or even coldly. They can only prosper in warmth, and soul warmth is enthusiasm. The spiritual content which is taken in like nutrition does not remain just content. It is reshaped because it interacts with that which is already present as insight. This process corresponds to the physical life process of *secretion (separation)*, better expressed in the case of taking in spiritual contents by the word *metamorphosis* or *transformation*. Then

23

the new content also serves the further *maintenance* of the conceptual organism. It *must* come to this, if this organism is to remain alive, or else it will wither away. Thus the conceptual organism does not stay the same, it *grows.* The most beautiful is actually *procreation,* the seventh life process, which truly works when the sentences of spiritual science are read correctly. The reader who nourishes his soul in this way brings forth something new. One hears from him not only the repetition of what he has read but knowledge that has been transformed and expanded, which cannot then be different in nature from the original source, because they originate from that source.

Thinker or Initiate?

There are a lot of people who judge Rudolf Steiner. When one says his name here in the Netherlands, mostly people ask: Isn't he that racist? Because the racism question is almost the only theme with which the name of Rudolf Steiner is associated publicly, a direct link is drawn to racism. People have also said to me: "Ah, that is the man with his three women!" Or: "He founded those schools where children remain illiterate, didn't he?" Rudolf Steiner is actually largely unknown in the world, and usually, one hears only such short-sighted, negative judgments about him, which only goes to prove what public opinion amounts to.

When, in an unprejudiced way, one lives into how people think about and experience Rudolf Steiner, one encounters all kinds of different feelings.

- There are the hastily formed judgments, in which Rudolf Steiner is felt to to be a deceiver of the people, the founder of a peculiar religion, an obnoxious mystic, a sectarian leader. 'Anthroposophers believe in reincarnation', 'they are all vegetarians, 'they all walk around in long skirts and sandals' etc.
- There are also people who feel that they have raised themselves intellectually far beyond 'that Steiner thing'. They are the 'true scientists' and have moved on far beyond the phase in which one believes in the spirit. These people also speak with contempt about Steiner, they do not believe a single word he says. In the common scientific literature one (almost) never finds a textual reference to Rudolf Steiner. When I realised this in the academic world when I wanted to write a thesis about Habermas

and Steiner, I was told: 'when you mention the name of Rudolf Steiner, all the doors of the academic world will close against you. One must be ashamed of Rudolf Steiner, he is considered as a dilettante, and is not taken seriously.'

- Then we have many people who stand in a spiritual stream that is not anthroposophical. Between 1994 and 2001 I held numerous lectures in new age centres and spiritual cafés about pure thinking as the necessary basis for spiritual development – whatever one's spiritual stream may be. However, thinking was and is always rejected in favour of the heart (or even the stomach). Rudolf Steiner is not considered to be a real spiritual master. It is all too complicated and 'head work', and that, they say, is precisely what must be overcome. Here one is also supposed to have gone far beyond Rudolf Steiner. Also, standing for Christ is seen as a relapse back into religious tradition which has been so splendidly surpassed by modern humanity.

- In the religious traditions themselves one is certainly not allowed to be a pupil of Steiner at all.

- And the anthroposophers? The followers of Rudolf Steiner? – The Anthroposophical Society is divided. There are loyal pupils who put the example of Rudolf Steiner above everything. There lurks the danger of idolization, in which one withdraws from normal life and does not carry through any real inner transformation that create new powers of life. A schema, a dead teacher, become intellectual icons and kill what is alive in pupils. One is deluded and is actually in a Society of deceased souls.

- A second type of anthroposopher one finds in those who are attracted by the enormous amount of knowledge in anthroposophy, but who can only handle it intellectually. To these people some contents of anthropo-

sophy are truly 'too ridiculous for words'; they imagine that Rudolf Steiner must have been mistaken on some points. A human being makes mistakes, they say, and so did that good old Rudolf Steiner. In the meantime, they claim, *we* have come way further, *our* scientific and moral insights will exceed those of Rudolf Steiner, so one should correct anthroposophy according to these new standards. One should free oneself of the Christian element in anthroposophy, for example, by concluding that Steiner only used the Christian concepts and images in order to reveal his spiritual insights in familiar forms. Actually, there is no Christ, He is only the shell within which the insights can be expressed. Thus, it becomes possible to assimilate anthroposophy with oriental paths of initiation. Or one liberates oneself from Christ in another way by being drawn to 'new initiates' such as Judith von Halle, but in fact, she only makes it more difficult for people to really understand the being of Christ.[5]
- Finally, even within the General Anthroposophical Society, we also have those who like to mock, whom one can find everywhere. In fact, they too think Rudolf Steiner is ridiculous, but because they also think that normal society is ridiculous, they mock it through 'being anthroposophers', while they mock Rudolf Steiner for his spiritual being, and his pupils for their respect.

Thus, one can find different 'essences' everywhere, one experiences Rudolf Steiner everywhere in various ways. He cannot show himself in his true being; the urn with his ashes rests on the hill in Dornach. He died in 1925. He is what others have made of him and make of him

---

5   See Mieke Mosmuller, *Stigmata und Geist-Erkenntnis* (Stigmata and Spiritual Knowledge), Occident 2008

still.

With the first three groups of people one cannot talk about Steiner and his anthroposophy at all. They are either completely uninterested, or else they are opponents. They have no interest, or they simply want to attack the figure of Rudolf Steiner still further. For these people, he is mostly not even a thinker, let alone an initiate. If one offers something from Rudolf Steiner to such people, it is tantamount to casting pearls before swine or to being torn apart by predators. The latter is easy to do to a human being that died such a long time ago: he cannot defend himself.

And the Society that is supposed to represent him and which could take his part and raise objections? It totally fails if it thinks that an open discussion is at all possible. One has the words 'publicity', 'openness', 'openness to the world' on one's lips but obviously does not know the principles of opinion-formation, does not know how words like 'discriminate' become rash *slogans* that penetrate deep into the feelings as negative-publicity and even deeper into the bodies of non-anthroposophers.

If Rudolf Steiner had only been a *thinker*, his thoughts and ideas could have been criticized with intellectual thinking. However, if he was an *initiate*, a 'supra-intellectual' thinking, a pure thinking would be required, and only through this could his statements be differentiated and tested. One would indeed not have to be an initiate oneself in order to be able to criticize Rudolf Steiner. Ordinary intellectual thinking, however, is too *dull,* too 'short-sighted', too bound up with words, to be able to measure up to the thinking of an initiate.

When one wants to present the thinking of Rudolf

Steiner to open criticism, one at least ought to seek to overcome *one's own* intellectual dullness.

Rudolf Steiner as thinker

With this book, I address everyone, who can summon up a genuine interest in a special personality, a man who has led a special life. That should be worth reading for everybody who is interested in people of special quality, at whatever level, whether he wants to live with anthroposophy or not. For that, we must for once totally forget what kind of feelings and judgments are formed inside us. As with a completely unknown man, we must approach him in an unprejudiced manner and experience all over again what makes itself visible to us. The anthroposopher too, who already 'knows' everything, would be able to join in this experience of *who* actually appears when one seeks to know Rudolf Steiner afresh.

Rudolf Steiner studied mathematics and natural sciences at the Technical University in Vienna. Besides that, he attended lectures on literature and was well versed in the philosophy of, among others, Kant and Fichte. Because of his friendship with his professor of German literature, Karl Julius Schröer, he made an in-depth study of the work of Goethe, including his writings on natural science. Insight into the spiritual work of Goethe thus arose in the young thinker, Rudolf Steiner. He gained insight into *how* Goethe's natural science, his theory of the metamorphosis of plants and his colour theory came into being. What became clearly perceptible to the young thinker in these studies was not only *what* insights Goethe had, but mainly *how* he came to them. Steiner was thus able to give shape to his first 'theory of knowledge': a 'theory of knowledge implicit in Goethe's world conception'. [6]

In this book we find a wonderfully ingenious explanation of the different levels of insight: for the physical (mineral) state of being, ordinary scientific thinking is sufficient. However, as soon as *life* enters into this (plant life), thinking must be reshaped in accordance with this, and this is also the case with animal life and human life.

Here, one already finds the beginnings of spiritual science, because it becomes very clear that one needs higher methods of thinking for higher modes of life. One can already feel in this book how natural scientific thinking becomes inadequate as soon as it wants to understand *life*.

From this theory of knowledge grew Rudolf Steiner's doctoral thesis: 'Wahrheit und Wissenschaft'[7] (Truth and Science). On the basis of the theories of knowledge of Kant and Fichte, he forms his own original theory of knowledge, which is not limited to a description of cognition but offers a view on moral freedom: ethical individualism.

In 'Truth and Science' for the first time he directs his philosophical attention in full consciousness on thinking itself and lets us participate in his experience that the creation of the category of cognition is a true rebirth in the spirit.

Although one already sees here the transition of Rudolf Steiner as thinker to Rudolf Steiner as initiate, everything takes place within thinking, and therefore every sensible, willing person can accompany him in the process.

---

[6]   Rudolf Steiner, *A Theory of Knowledge Implicit in Goethe's World Conception with Special Reference to Schiller*, GA 2

[7]   Rudolf Steiner, *Truth and Science*, GA 3

It is important to hold in one's inner contemplation this transitional point: from Rudolf Steiner as thinker to Rudolf Steiner as initiate. When we want to understand his living being in its relationship to living anthroposophy, it is this very point that must be fathomed clearly and focused on contemplatively.

Previously, Rudolf Steiner had already philosophized epistemologically, he had understood the principles of Goethe's theory of knowledge, while Goethe himself had 'never thought about thinking' and had not striven after that. However, Rudolf Steiner understood it, and this can be called a veritable 'thinking about thinking'. Although Rudolf Steiner had the spiritual work of Goethe before his thinker's eye, and not his own work, still it was a complete 'thinking about thinking'. I leave out of consideration here the question of whether Steiner was already an initiate (before 1892). It is certain that he was able to view spiritual reality at that time. I do not want to refer to external facts here, but only address myself to the work of Rudolf Steiner, from which his spiritual figure nevertheless should come forward most clearly – when one is able to read it in the right way. He did not write as an initiate in these years, but as a thinker. He had thought through and lived through the way in which Goethe came to his way of knowledge, and consequently discovered how this spirit acted, how it worked differently when he concerned himself with physical (mineral) phenomena from when he busied himself with studying the world of plants etc.

In 'Truth and Science', his philosophical thesis, Rudolf Steiner concentrates on the theory of knowledge in general. In Fichte he discovers a man who can almost totally see through human knowing and the human I, but who, however, does not come to the ultimate conclusion. This ultimate conclusion is that the human I brings about itself, when it acknowledges itself. The human I is able to understand cognition, *because* it accomplishes it itself. The I can know what cognition is because it is cognition itself. Thus it is actual self-knowledge that is awakened here. But at the same time, philosophy is hereby made redundant, it has burnt itself up and gives rise to a new form: this resurrected philosophy is anthroposophy, because it is human self-knowledge in the original sphere of wisdom, but now achieved to its full extent.

Rudolf Steiner does not use the word anthroposophy in 'Truth and Science'. However, one can conceive of it already in reading, when he lets this anthroposophy shine through in the following sentence[8]:

> *'The circumstance that the I can engage freely in activity, makes it possible for it, by itself, to realize the category of cognition through self-determination, while in the rest of the world the categories reveal themselves to be connected through objective necessity with what is the given and which corresponds to them.'[9]*

The I is truly born for the first time right here. Previously, it was the soul (the Intellectual Soul) that formed the thoughts. It formed them by means of a 'thinking instinct', without awareness of what it actually does. The I only steps forward out of the soul when it loosens itself from the soul, rouses itself and asks questions about cognition itself.

> *'But the concept and the given reality of consciousness are originally separated, from which separation is derived the connection between them, and therefore cognition is of the nature that we have de-*

---

[8] Nb p. 85 in the 1981 Steinerbooks edition of *Truth and Science*.

[9] Ibid., p.83

scribed. Because the Idea and the given inevitably appear separately in consciousness, the whole of reality splits in two, and because consciousness can connect these two elements only through its own activity, it only achieves full reality through the act of cognition. All other categories (Ideas) are necessarily connected to the corresponding forms of the given, even when they are not comprehended through cognition, but it is only through conscious activity that the Idea of cognition can be united with the given that corresponds to it. Consciousness as reality only exists when it realizes itself.[10]

The first cognitive act by this I is knowing itself as a thinking, cognizing being, and this acknowledging of itself as a thinking, cognitive being is original; it can not be passed on (adopted), but has to be 'done' by the I independently. With this, the soul is fertilized by the spirit. The category of cognition is added to the object (the cognitive process). This step, which can not be regarded and experienced highly enough, already shines through between the lines of 'Truth and Science'. Here one has definitely not to do with only 'thinking', with ideas, notions, judgments or whatever. Here it is about an actual *step* in the development of one's consciousness; it is about a realization of one's own spiritual being. This being subsequently *is present*; the human being has become new, resurrected. No-one in history except Rudolf Steiner has ever formulated this act of consciousness in· thinking. This should be thoroughly *experienced* by one who has fully understood the content of this book thus far. In this experiencing one comes to a first meeting with the living Rudolf Steiner.

Can one not become tremendously inspired by this? Does one miss it while reading? If the human being himself is not capable yet of actually taking this step of consciousness, he

---

[10]   Ibid., p.72

can at least *imagine* what such a realization would mean. In Rudolf Steiner's biography after this point one sees this meaning unfold. The 'ordinary' human being, however, the reader, the pupil ... can he not imagine this step? Can he plunge into his own living thinking process and experience the indisputable truth in his imagination? Can he not then wish to follow this with all of his will, because it is clear to him, that every human being is able to? Because the time is right for it? Because the great spiritual personalities of earlier times have paved the way for this ability inside us?

The intellect resists this realization; it only wants to know passively, to be acknowledged eventually. It absolutely does not want to move on to deeds, to willing. A meditative experiencing of any phrase from 'Truth and Science' would be able to heal this disease, would already cure it in the process of experiencing.

Then, although philosophy had already given way to anthroposophy, followed Rudolf Steiner's main work of philosophy, 'The Philosophy of Freedom'. [11]

What began in 'Truth and Science' as a theme, becomes a whole composition in two parts in 'the Philosophy of Freedom': the science or knowledge of freedom and the reality of freedom.

In the first part, the concept of freedom is developed on the basis 'that the I can transform itself actively in freedom, in order to realize the category of cognizing', by means of insight in the cognitive process, step by step (which was to be expected). *If* one finally transforms the I, in freedom, into activity, then it has wakened from the soul and stands

---

[11]   Rudolf Steiner, *The Philosophy of Freedom*, GA 4

free outside the soul, which is still connected to the body. *Then* freedom has become actual. In the free I morality glows, it comes into consciousness in the form of the moral Idea. However, it can realize itself, it can become perceptible in free moral acts, which the human being accomplishes in freedom on the base of his awakened I. What was previously a realization inside himself, in which the self was born through his own activity, now grows in the world, where freedom becomes 'perceptible', becomes reality. Freedom realizes itself, acts are accomplished that lie beyond the order of nature, but also beyond karma. In that sense they are real *miracles*, because they actually cannot be accomplished, but are nevertheless. They were not counted on; a new world has arisen.

However, a side effect makes its appearance. The human being, who tries in the above-mentioned manner to understand freedom (the science of freedom) and thus realize it (the reality of freedom) must become internally active. Understanding does not succeed with a passive state of mind. One could perhaps repeat the content once more, even analyze and combine it, but that is not *understanding*. Conception only arises when the I transforms itself into activity in freedom, in order actually to know what knowing is. Here, reading must be replaced by something else. It cannot just remain reading, however lively it may be. It must become a genuine imitation. The thinking soul can imitate what it finds described as processes. It is something that one can perform *after* reading. First, one has read actively and absorbed the knowing processes in one's thinking. Then, however, one tries to really examine in oneself what is written there. Is one able to perceive one's thinking? Or does it escape one's attention time and again? One can *do* such a thing within oneself.

Therefore, one must accomplish the labour of Hercules, a labour that seems to be an impossible task, to perceive one's own face without a mirror. But within oneself, this is possible. Does there exist a more solid ground for trust in Rudolf Steiner's deeds of knowledge, as a realization of one's own I? If it *works* it must be true... Then the whole world can turn against it and declare that it is all nonsense – but one knows better and is silent, or ultimately, declares the truth of this reality, even if it is a cry in solitude. ...

This internally developed activity of the I that anyone can develop through this labour of Hercules, begins to become an independent 'side effect'. It is no longer only perceived as content, but begins to work inside of you; it becomes something living. You begin to feel the cognitive process as a force, a movement, a moving energy, a strength that can fill itself with light and love. You feel yourself in the 'I', but this 'I' is threefold: strength, light and love. The more one comes to the point of experiencing oneself outside the cognitive processes of daily life – as a spectator who participates from a position that one normally never takes in thinking - thus in a exceptional state – the more powerfully strength fills itself with light and love.

This is the 'side effect' of serious work with Rudolf Steiner's 'Philosophy of Freedom', which still shows Rudolf Steiner as a thinker but as one who already has within him the potential of initiation.

For Rudolf Steiner himself this difference between thinker and initiate applies in another way. For us, he steps forward as an initiate just after the turn of the century. When one wants to follow him, one finds a sure path to the spirit in the sequence of his writings. But the human being Rudolf Steiner stood already fully in the spiritual world in his young years. He says so himself in the lecture cycle about the requisite self-awareness of anthroposophers: 'the history and the conditions of the anthroposophical movement in relation to the Anthroposophical Society.'[12]

'I might perhaps say: by these observations of life that I wish to tell you about as an introduction to the history of the anthroposophical movement, I must emphasize that for me, at the time[13] when I was brought by destiny to these observations, my connection to the spiritual world, how I stood within this spiritual world, was never cut off. The spiritual world was always present. I must underline this, because it must form the background of my account of these observations: the spiritual world as self-evident, and the people on earth seen as the images of that what they actually are as spiritual beings in the spiritual world. I want to characterize this state of feeling, so that you always presume this as the spiritual background.

Naturally, this observing was not an observing with a dog's wet nose, but with a warm-hearted participation, without wanting to be an observer, in that one was always right inside things – in all friendliness, sociability and politeness of course.'

---

[12]   Rudolf Steiner, GA 258, p.20
[13]   The end of the 80s in the 19th century

Rudolf Steiner between thinker and initiate

Beside the afore-mentioned books there also exists a quantity of other literature in the form of essays and articles, among others from the time before the turn of the century. Because the outward characteristic of Rudolf Steiner was that he had the ability to think along and feel along with others enthusiastically, and that he was also very gifted, one can experience him from many angles in these writings. So he has been seen as follower of Nietzsche, a supporter of Haeckel's evolutionary theories, an anarchist, an opponent of Christianity etc. He could take on any form, so to speak, and it is often hard for some to follow the thread. Nevertheless, when one sticks to his theory of knowledge, one develops the skill *oneself* to think along with all his thoughts, and one can genuinely see the thread very clearly and understand it too. Then every expression becomes part of this versatile personality and shows a human being that took in and reflected the whole world-soul of that time.

One does not have to take blindly what he says and writes, one can simply leave it to *Rudolf Steiner's* responsibility. Only dogmatists have to answer for their dogmas. A free man does not have to apologize for the statements of another free man. He knows that the free man reflects more deeply on his statements than the unfree man and thus knows that these free statements of free people are perfectly understandable. However, one must not surrender to the lack of freedom of public opinion. Judgments are widely prevalent there which are not intelligent and spiritual enough to bring about free statements or appreciate these statements. Thus, when a contemporary Anthroposophical Society wants to apologize for statements that Rudolf

Steiner has made, it shows itself to be a dogmatic sectarian association in doing so. Or else it has striven *itself* finally to free itself from this Master of the Occident by pulling this master down to its own spiritless level.

In this book I try to paint the spiritual figure of Rudolf Steiner. It appears in the dynamic of his mastership.

I will be criticized as a worshipper of Rudolf Steiner. However, I am a free individual in this, who has acknowledged the grandeur of this man through the *effects* of his work. I do not need to apologize for my enthusiasm or to take up his knowing as dogma. His knowledge proves itself, when it can become alive in us.

Rudolf Steiner himself describes the actual change from thinker to initiate in chapter XX of 'Chapters in the Course of My Life'. In this chapter – that for everyone who searches for the living Rudolf Steiner must be a source of knowledge – he describes the change from an experiencing of ideas to a true experiencing of the spirit:[14]

'I felt how the ideal thinking that I had practised till then withdrew in a certain direction and was replaced by an element of will. To make this possible, the will must be able to hold at bay all subjective capriciousness in the unfolding of cognition. The will increased to the degree that the ideal decreased. And the will also took over the spiritual knowing that previously was almost totally accomplished by the ideal. I had already realized that the threefold disposition of the soul life in thinking, feeling and willing only had a limited meaning. In reality, inside thinking, feeling and willing is present, but thinking is the most prevalent. In feeling lives thinking and

---

14   Rudolf Steiner, *The Course of My life*, GA 28, p.327f

willing, and in willing, likewise, lives thinking and feeling. Now it became clear to me how willing took in more of thinking, and thinking more of willing.

Meditating leads, on the one hand, to a knowing of the spiritual, but on the other hand, the consequence of such self-observation is the inner strengthening of the spiritual human being who is independent of the organism and the confirmation of his being in the spiritual world, just as the physical human being has his confirmation in the physical world. He becomes aware how the confirmation of the spiritual human being in the spiritual world increases immeasurably when the physical organism does not limit this confirmation while the physical organism's confirmation of itself in the physical world gives way to disintegration - in death – when the spiritual human being is no longer able to maintain this confirmation from out of himself.'

Then he describes, how he had his Christ-experience in that same period of his life several years later (around the turn of the century). The change from the experiencing of ideas to the experiencing of the spirit lies around his 36th year of his life, thus around 1897. Several years later, he finds Christ, observing him in the mystery of Golgotha, 'as a mystical fact'.[15]

'It was in that period, in which the actual content of my statements about Christianity so contradicted what I would later say about it, that the real content (of Christianity) began to unfold, seed-like, before my soul as an inner phenomenon of knowledge. Around the turn of the century the kernel steadily unfolded within me. Before the turn of the century occurred the previously-mentioned testing of the soul. My soul had arrived at the point of standing before the Mystery of

---

[15]   Ibid., p.366

43

Golgotha in a most inward, solemn celebration of knowledge.'

In this time therefore lies the completion of the transition from thinker to initiate, which also shows itself in the style of the two books that he subsequently publishes: 'Mysticism at the Dawn of the Modern Age'[16] and 'Christianity as Mystical Fact'. [17]

The preface in 'Mysticism at the Dawn of the Modern Age' is, above all, a miracle in itself. Through the philosophy of freedom the I is born as a perceptible force by bringing about its own exceptional state as an observer of the process of thinking and its own activity. It still finds itself wholly in the thinking of thinking, in a thinking which is observed. In the preface of this next book it becomes clear that the exceptional state of the I corresponds to a *new sense* that makes everything that was already present in the soul appear in a splendid new form. Rudolf Steiner describes with great clarity how everything noble had always been observed with this sense, and with Fichte he says: *'what is new is that this sense is able to see itself'.* This resembles the formula Steiner had already written in 'Truth and Knowledge', but now in the sense of modern initiation. Who wakens this new sense inside himself, experiences internal resurrection, through which everything can be observed in a completely new light. Here one clearly finds expressed, how philosophy changes into anthroposophy, now no longer only in the realm of freedom but as a fact of initiation.

Also, anyone who has a keen interest in modern initia-

---

16   Rudolf Steiner, GA 7

17   Rudolf Steiner, GA 8

tion should experience what is written there meditatively, meditate on it experientially and try to imitate it. Only then does one get an idea of the living Rudolf Steiner. [18]

'In self-knowledge they saw the opening up of a new sense. And in their opinion this sense leads to insights which do not exist for one who does not perceive in self-knowledge that which differentiates it from all other kinds of knowing. One to whom this sense has not opened itself thinks that self-knowledge arises in a way similar to knowledge through external senses, or through some other means acting from the outside. He thinks, "Knowledge is knowledge". However, in one case its object is something situated in the external world, in the other case it is in his own soul. He hears only words, at best abstract thoughts, in what, for those who look deeper, constitutes the basis of their inner life namely, in the dictum that in all other kinds of knowing the object is outside of ourselves, while in self-knowledge we stand inside the object; that every other object comes into contact with us as something completed and closed, while in our self we actively and creatively weave what we observe in ourselves. This may appear as an explanation consisting of mere words, perhaps as a triviality, but if properly understood, it can also appear as a higher light which illuminates all other knowledge in a new way. He to whom it appears under the first aspect is in the same situation as a blind man to whom one says, a brilliant object is there. He hears the words, but for him brilliance does not exist. One can unite in oneself the sum of the knowledge of a period; if one does not perceive the significance of self-knowledge then in the higher sense all knowledge is but blind.

Independent of us, the world lives for us because it communicates itself to our spirit. What is communicated to us must be expressed in the language characteristic of us. A book would be meaningless for

[18] Rudolf Steiner, GA 7, p.18f

us if its contents were to be presented to us in an unknown tongue. In the same way the world would be meaningless for us if it did not speak to us in our language. The same language which reaches us from the realm of objects, we also hear in ourselves. But then it is we who are speaking. It is only a matter of listening aright to the transformation which occurs when we close our perception to external objects and listen only to that which then sounds in ourselves. It is for this that the new sense is necessary. If it is not awakened we think that in the communications about ourselves we perceive only communications about an object external to ourselves; we are of the opinion that there is something hidden somewhere which speaks to us in the same way as do external objects. If we have the new sense we know that its perceptions are quite different from those which refer to external objects. Then we know that this sense does not leave outside of itself that which it perceives, as the eye leaves outside of itself the object it sees, but that it can completely incorporate its object within itself. If I see an object, the object remains outside of me; if I perceive myself, I myself enter into my perception. One who seeks some part of his self outside what is perceived, shows that the essential content of what is perceived has not become apparent to him.

Initiation in Christ

There are no extant descriptions of Rudolf Steiner's Christian initiation. There do exist oral statements, two written paragraphs, and there is the whole work of Rudolf Steiner, which makes it very evident that he was a Christian initiate. He wrote no book in which he clearly described the precise steps he took, and how his Christ experience came about. One has to read and feel all this through the lines – and one can experience it in the extensive number of his books and the sheer amount of his activities. These point to a super-human force, a force that a human being can not have only from his own nature.

In 'The Course of My Life' Rudolf Steiner describes the development of his thinking – the questions with which he struggled, the answers that he found. However, the book does not give direct information about what he achieved when, or how far his development had actually progressed by a certain time. In a letter that he wrote when he was a young adult (1881), he reveals frankly that he had the all-embracing experience of the I in one night.[19]

'It was the night of the 10ᵗʰ to 11ᵗʰ of January, when I did not sleep at all. I had been busy with a philosophical problem until twelve thirty at night, when I finally went to bed; my effort last year was to study if it was true what Schelling says: 'Inside all of us lives a secret, a wonderful ability to retrieve our naked self from the changing experience of time within us and from all that comes to us from the outside world and there in the form of the unchanging observe

---

19   Christoph Lindenberg, Rudolf Steiner, Rowohlt 1992

eternity within us.' I believed and still believe that I have discovered that inner ability inside me – for I had sensed it already for a long time; the whole idealistic philosophy stands before me now in an essential, modified form; what is a sleepless night compared to such a discovery!'

The second place is the passage quoted below from 'The Course of My Life', in which Rudolf Steiner gives evidence of his having 'stood before the Mystery of Golgotha'. He was then at the end of his thirties.

The letter in which he writes about the experience of his I probably describes his first actual Christ-experience, although he obviously did not see it as such at that time.[20]

Contrary to what I wrote about Christianity later, there are a number of statements that I wrote down and made in my lectures at that time. Related to that there is the following consideration. Whenever I wrote down the word 'Christianity' at that time, I had in mind the religious doctrine of the hereafter which permeated the Christian confessions. Every content of the religious experience pointed to a spiritual world that would not be accessible through the unfolding of one's spiritual forces. What religion has to say and what she has to offer as moral commands derives from revelations that come to man from the outside. My view of the spirit resisted that; it wanted to experience the spiritual world just as much as the sense world through observable perceptions in man and in nature. My ethical individualism also resisted it; it did not want the moral life to be based on any external commands, but from the development of the psychological-spiritual human being, in which the divine lives.

...

[20] Rudolf Steiner, GA 28, p.363 and 365f

'In thinking that can develop itself from natural science – but did not at that time – I saw the basis on which mankind could reach to insight in the spiritual world. Therefore I put the accent very strongly on knowledge of the foundations of nature, which should lead to spiritual knowledge. For the one who does not, like me, stand with his experiences in the spiritual world, going in a certain direction of thinking merely signifies being active in thinking. But for the one who experiences the spiritual world, it means something essentially different. He is brought into the proximity of beings in the spiritual world that want to make such a direction of thinking absolutely sovereign. One-sidedness in knowledge is not only the cause of abstract errors; it leads to a spiritually lively association with beings, which represents error in the human world. Later, I spoke about ahrimanic beings when I wanted to point in this direction. For them it is an absolute reality that the world should become a machine. They live in a world that borders directly on the sense world.

Not for a moment I have been a prey to this world. Neither in my subconsciousness, because I maintained a very careful watch over all my cognitive acts so that they would all occur in clear consciousness. All the more conscious was also my internal struggle against the demonic powers that did not want to develop a spiritual observation from natural science, but only a mechanical-materialistic way of thinking.

The one that seeks spiritual knowledge must experience this world; merely thinking about it theoretically is not enough for him. At that time I had to save my spiritual sight amidst storms within me. These storms formed the background of my outer life.

In this time of testing, it was only possible for me to come further when, with my spiritual sight I turned back to the development of Christianity and put it before my soul. That led to the knowledge that I brought to expression in my book 'Christianity as Mystical

49

Fact'. Before that time, I had always pointed to a Christian content that lived in the existing confessions of faith. Nietzsche did that too.

In an earlier place in this biography (page 48ff.) I describe a conversation about Christ that I had with an erudite Cistercian priest who was also a professor in Vienna at the Catholic Theological faculty. In him I encountered a sceptical state of mind. I did not find the Christianity that I was searching for anywhere in the confessions of faith. After I was exposed to a heavy soul struggle at the time of the testing, I had to go into Christianity myself, and indeed in that world in which the spirit speaks about it.

From my stance towards Christianity, it becomes totally clear how, in spiritual science, I did not seek and find anything on the path that many people ascribe to me. They represent the matter so as to say that I have combined elements of spiritual knowledge from old traditions, as if I had reworked Gnostic and other teachings. What was gained in the way of spiritual knowledge in 'Christianity as Mystical Fact' derives directly from the spiritual world. It was only to demonstrate to audiences at lectures and to readers of the book how the spirituality observed is consistent with historical traditions that I wrote about the latter and gave them a place in the content. But I did not add anything from these documents to the content that I had not observed beforehand in the spirit.

'It was in that period, in which the actual content of my statements about Christianity so contradicted what I would later say about it, that the real content (of Christianity) began to unfold, seed-like, before my soul as an inner phenomenon of knowledge. Around the turn of the century the kernel steadily unfolded within me. Before the turn of the century occurred the previously-mentioned testing of the soul. My soul had arrived at the point of standing before the Mystery of Golgotha in a most inward, solemn celebration of knowledge.'

It is very clear that Rudolf Steiner fought for his own spiritual position in the midst of the greatest contradiction between outer Christianity and true Christian experience. Therefore he first needed to live through the transformation from thinker to initiate. He described this clearly in 'The Course of My Life':[21]

> *In connection to the change in my soul life I went through very difficult inner experiences. In my soul experience I understood the being of meditation and its meaning for insight into the spiritual world. Previously, I had also led a meditative life; but the impulse for that derived from idealistic knowledge as to the value of meditation for a spiritual world-view. Now something stirred internally, as a result of which meditation became a necessity for the existence of my soul life. The soul life I had attained needed meditation like the organism at a certain step of its development needs to breathe through the lungs.*
>
> *The connection between normal conceptual knowledge from sense perception and the perception of the spirit advanced for me at that time in my life from a more ideal experience to an experience in which the whole human being takes part in. Ideal experience, which however takes up into itself what is really spiritual, is the element from which my Philosophy of Freedom was born. Experience by the whole human being includes the spiritual world in a much more vital way than ideal experience. And yet the latter is already a higher step compared to a conceptual grasp of the sense world. In ideal experience one does not grasp the sense world, but a spiritual world that, as it were, borders directly on the sense world.*
> *When all that was searching in my soul for expression and experience at that time, I was aware of three types of knowledge within me. The first type is conceptual knowledge, which is acquired by*

21   Ibid., p.323ff

sense perception. The soul appropriates it and retains it internally in accordance with one's existing strength of memory. Repeating the content that is taken in, is only meaningful for memorising it well. With the second type of knowledge no concepts are acquired in relation to sense perception, but they are experienced independently from the senses. The experience warrants through its own being that the concepts are founded in a spiritual reality. With this type of knowledge the same certainty applies as with sense knowledge, when one knows that one has no illusions but physical reality in front of one.

With this ideal-spiritual knowledge it is already not sufficient anymore – as with sense-based knowledge – that one acquires it with the result that it becomes a possession of the memory. The process of acquiring it must become continuous. Just as it is not sufficient for the organism to breathe for a while in order subsequently to use the breath for the further life process, thus is the form of knowledge acquisition that applies to sense-based knowledge insufficient for this ideal-spiritual type of knowledge. To this end, it is necessary that the soul remains in a permanent, living interaction with the world in which one transposes oneself through this knowledge. This happens through meditation, which – as indicated earlier – originates from ideal insight into the value of meditating. I searched for this interaction already long before my soul change (in the 35th year of my life).

Now meditating became a life necessity for the soul. And because of this, arose the third type of knowledge within me. It did not only lead to further depths of the spiritual world, but also resulted in an intimate living together with it.

After this metamorphosis he had to rescue his spirit-observation in internal soul struggle ('storms'). It was in this time of testing that he formed his spiritual perception of the development of Christianity, and about that he says the words previously quoted.

From this time on, everything that Rudolf Steiner taught, was embedded in this Christ-experience, even when he did not speak about it. Thus it was the other way round: he did not use the Christ-Event as an 'image' for illumining things; rather, Christ lived in everything he said, even when the content of what he taught was completely different.

A musical human being experiences musically, even when there is no music to be heard. He recognizes what is musical as soon as it lets itself be experienced – in whatever circumstances.

In 'The Mysticism...' Christian mystics are discussed, but also Spinoza and Fichte. It is with 'Christianity as Mystical Fact' that for the first time Steiner describes the experience of the Christ-Event as a *fact*. Perhaps the reader does not find what he is looking for in this book; perhaps he does not find Christ, because only the 'being of the fact' is described. Then the reader must meditate on sections of the book, so that they will deepen to experience. Thus he finds what he is looking for – and knows from that moment on, that the writer writes from 'having found Christ'.

One who wants to find Christ must go to great pains. Because He leaves the human being free. He only shows Himself when costs are borne and efforts made – only then has man proven his free choice.

Christian Theosophy

Rudolf Steiner became the teacher for the German Theosophical Society. He agreed to this, because he wanted to do justice to Marie von Sivers' question about an esotericism for the Occident. From the outset, it was clear that he wanted to establish a new road in Theosophy: the Christian esoteric path. But he could not teach in a different language and thus he had to use the words that were common in Theosophy. He therefore embodied his Christian knowledge in theosophical language.

He is often accused of merely distorting old esoteric knowledge and teaching it as if it were something new and original. Such accusations can only be made by lazy people. Because what matters here is that one who keeps on actively meditating on Rudolf Steiner's spirit-knowledge grows into a living, weaving, multi-form, panoramic world-word. Amazed, one will at least wonder how it is possible that *one* man is steeped in such knowledge. One will no longer doubt for a second or think it *impossible* that a *single* human being has carried such knowledge. Like a concert pianist stands above the separate musical notes and makes them all audible in a musical work of art, so has this artist gone beyond the separate facts of knowledge. This early theosophy of Rudolf Steiner is no combined, composed knowledge, but a Christ-word embodied in normal theosophical language.

Thus the book 'Theosophy'[22] was published, in which for

---

[22]   Rudolf Steiner, *Theosophy*, GA 9

the first time man appears in his four-, seven-, and even ninefoldness; in which the path of the soul and spiritual after death is described; in which karma and reincarnation are spoken of; and in which mainly the path is described that every human being can take who seeks initiation. It becomes very clear that man must clear his soul for that and that he must become master over all his unconscious urges. No effortless enlightenment in front of the computer screen[23] awaits man, but continuously stringent practice – it cannot be deep and stringent enough. And because it is unspoken yet very clear that the writer of this 'Theosophy' meets all these requirements himself, he does not appear as a genius thinker or natural clairvoyant but steps forward as a holy man. It does not have to be that such a saint is completely perfect, it is not about that at all. It is about the permanent will to self-perfection. Holiness is not an acquired perfection, but a *striving* for perfection.

At the same time Rudolf Steiner gave lectures and held esoteric classes. The documentation of these describes them in an incomplete way, and one sees how Rudolf Steiner dresses his knowledge there in theosophical words. But in the written books his independent spirit-knowledge presents itself clearly as an occidental process of knowledge. To it can be applied the phrase 'Ex Occidente Lux', which defines a veritable science of the Grail.

---

[23]   Sebastian Gronbach, *Missionen* (Missions), 2008

Knowledge of the Higher Worlds – How Is It Achieved?

The contemporary human being today, who is only capable of perceiving things intellectually or subjectively, has lost the ability to form a lively image in his soul of a description he receives. This means that a biography only calls up a vague impression of the person portrayed, certainly not a living one. When it is written therefore that Rudolf Steiner stood in front of the mystery of Golgotha in a solemn celebration of knowledge, that is a row of words with a concept in them. One can accept it as true or not. If one does not accept it as true, one does not actually have to engage with Rudolf Steiner anymore, unless one has the urge to demolish his greatness. If one doubts - and that is always justified – one can go deeply into everything relating to anthroposophy and Rudolf Steiner, and the truth will appear. When somehow one comes to a certain conviction that Rudolf Steiner actually did stand before the Mystery of Golgotha, one should not merely pass by this sentence but imagine in as lively a manner as possible how a man, in fact, really, with his soul and his spirit, stood before Christ and experienced Christ's Deed. Not simply read further, but let the sentence become an imagination, an image; one has to muster courage for this. And not only one such a sentence has to be read and experienced like this; all of Rudolf Steiner's work deserves such attention and devotion.

Only a few readers read in this way, but nevertheless, others allow themselves to pass through a sentence rapidly, making judgments as they go: true, disputable, untrue, nonsense etc. That is also the way we handle each other, without respect, making quick judgments. But in social life judgments are often adjusted. Conflicts arise, and the judgment is rectified by reality. A person that is no longer among the living cannot work in this way anymore; he has to put up with everything, he can indeed inspire people alive on earth, but cannot not speak for himself. That is why the responsibility of the reader is much greater. He must feel that he has to hold back his judgment and that he has to try to make a reality out of what he has read. Then one gets a deep, deeply moving image of what it means to have 'stood before the Mystery of Golgotha'. From this moment on, Rudolf Steiner stands in a very different light. One gets a sort of memory, when one sees this human being standing before the cross, a memory of a devout monk, a man, who at that time, ages earlier, was already a saintly man through and through, a man in whom at that time a profound love for Christ had already been realised. This relationship resurrected in Rudolf Steiner and is lived through again with the fully developed spiritual soul, but in the background one 'sees', experiences this silent, devout, famous monk. At that time already as holy as an angel, and despite that, as erudite as a doctor, even a professor. Now in the transition from the 19th to the 20th century, the love for Christ is renewed, but the present time does not allow for external glory. He would become famous, but not acknowledged by the world.

Standing spiritually before the Mystery of Golgotha ... for the one who dares to experience this in his marrow, Rudolf Steiner is a Master from that moment on - the Master with the task of preaching the 'Ex Occidente Lux', the light that glows in the Holy Grail. He is the Master of the Occident.

His essays on the path of initiation are published in bookform as: 'Knowledge of the Higher Worlds – How Is It Achieved?'. Step by step, the inner schooling is described. Above all, however, it is the moral conditions that are described. From this description it becomes clear that the man who attains this initiation does not only have to purify his soul completely, but that above all, he has to gain full mastery over the capacities of his soul and spirit. One who is initiated does not only have his desires and instincts under control, but also his feelings and sensations, his every thought, the true connection between his thoughts and the observed world, all his sense impressions, spiritual images, inspirations, intuitions.

And now we place before ourselves the same demand as before: as clearly, strongly and extensively as possible, we imagine Rudolf Steiner as initiate. What qualities does he have? He is, in the light of full consciousness, master of his instincts and desires and he is master of his entire life of soul and spirit: feelings, thoughts, sense impressions etc. If that was not the case, he would be a deceiver, a bad teacher. But if we comprehend that he actually was an initiate, we must conclude the above. One must really make for oneself an intensive imagination of this man, and not look over it quickly. One must not feel jealous, but let oneself be touched by the experience. Behind this man we see the holiness of his thoughts in earlier incarnations. Now we see a man in whom these holy thoughts have truly become soul skills. Can one not feel a deep respect for that, without praising *the man*?

What is given as a range of ideas in Rudolf Steiner's 'Philosophy of Freedom', returns in a higher and deeper shape in 'Knowledge of the Higher Worlds – How Is It Achieved?'[24] Therefore it is harder to follow the path than in 'Truth and Science' and 'Philosophy of Freedom'. Be-

---

[24]   Rudolf Steiner, GA 10

cause there one only had to do with pure thinking and the attainment of the special, exceptional state that belongs to that. But here we actually have to already have acquired these skills. For who in the bustle of everyday life has the self-conscious force to summon up the ability to face the world and its phenomena in a mood of reverence? In order to be able to do so, one has to be able to foster one's thinking in purity. And who can loosen himself from his own subjectivity so strongly that he can observe an event in his own biography from the outside? Therefore, one has to be experienced in adopting the exceptional state, stepping out of himself. What is already difficult in one's inmost feelings becomes an impossibility in daily life. Perhaps it would still have been possible at the beginning of the 20th century, when daily life was not yet so hectic as it is today. But in our time it becomes increasingly impossible to have such a strong self-consciousness without making prior effort to attain pure thinking.

It is known that pupils of Rudolf Steiner who embarked on the path had to admit, astonished, that there were long, very long distances between the different stages of initiation. The individuality that was Rudolf Steiner was already so advanced on this path that he was no longer visible. Then the danger is that such a man is placed above everyone as uniquely gifted; or that such development as his is considered to be impossible for ordinary mortals to achieve; that the pupil looses courage or gives up his striving in disappointment, or starts to challenge the teacher. Of course, that all happened, and it still happens. The discouraged pupil can also take other paths, for example, return to the church or choose different spiritual paths. We must under no condition be paralysed. The teacher does not have to disappear from our field of view. We can always place him again in our field of view and let his development work as an ideal. We find how one must guide one's steps extensively described in 'Knowledge of the Higher Worlds – How Is It Achieved?'

Occult Science – An Outline

In 1909 a comprehensive 'textbook' appeared that contained the most important insights of esoteric science. When one wants to experience Rudolf Steiner as a living individuality instead of as a picture on the wall, as a statue in the bookcase, as an often-mentioned or quoted scholar, one must read and meditate on this book in real connection with the writer. By that, I do not mean that the writer and the book are one and the same, but that we must make ourselves conscious from time to time, that a human being (Rudolf Steiner) has received this science and described it. If we don't do this, then we shall gradually forget who we actually had to do with at the establishing of anthroposophy, and then the peeling away of anthroposophy from its teacher takes place, the separation that we see everywhere these days. But that must not be, because spiritual science as merely knowledge that is handed down, without a connection to Rudolf Steiner, will become a bait for the intellect that is only able to analyse and combine; indeed, this has already happened.

What is being said here is something other than the affirmation of blind faith in a teacher; that would work just as destructively. Because the free man must make esoteric science his own by independent pure thinking, he must stand alone completely, remain free from judgements. Moreover, the above-mentioned consciousness must be cultivated that there was a man, who observed all this himself and has put it in words understandable for the intellect! In the 'Introduction' to the first edition (1909) Rudolf Steiner writes about the attitude he expects from his pupils:[25]

The author wishes to state plainly: he would like readers who are not content to take on blind faith the matters presented here, but who will make the effort to put them to the test of their own soul's insight and experience of life. He only wants cautious readers, who will only let themselves be convinced by the logically justifiable.'

Therefore, he naturally needs readers who can exercise pure thinking, in order to allow this - which can only justify things logically - to apply. Common judgments are mostly insufficient for this because they are simply *not cautious*.

The cautious reader must thus create his conviction of the truth of what is presented from his knowledge that what is presented can be logically justified. This belief would at the same time be an acknowledgment of the ability of the writer – that would also be logically justified.

But there is another possibility: namely, not wanting to see as logically justified that Rudolf Steiner is a great initiate, because most of *Occult Science - An Outline* contains knowledge that was already known, only not publicly. Theosophy knew of it, and after Rudolf Steiner's death, in 1930, writings of Mani (215-277) were discovered, in which the origins of the earth had been described in a similar way. Rudolf Steiner could not have drawn from these writings; however, they show that this occult science is already very ancient.

---

25   Rudolf Steiner, *Occult Science – An Outline*, GA 13

Mani:

'You know that there are seven earth spheres.'

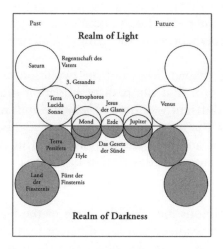

Rudolf Steiner repeatedly explained that he did not teach anything that he did not acknowledge in the spirit, and had observed in the spiritual world. If he was not an absolute liar – and we must already have determined the truth of that for ourselves earlier – it follows that he had himself observed the content of the chapter 'Man and the Evolution of the World'. If one holds Rudolf Steiner to be a liar, it does not make sense to occupy oneself with his writings any longer. But if one acknowledges him as one who speaks the truth, then one knows that he has observed the contents of *Occult Science* himself. That this observation gives rise to contents that were already known in some form need not surprise us, because it is the very characteristic of truth that it does not reveal itself in only *one way*.

It is in this way that the process of knowledge must shape itself inside us. On the one hand, we must think through the content and experience that the content is logically justified; on the other hand, we must deeply experience from time to time that there *was* a real author of this occult science – so that not only does an occult science grow within us, but also an experience of the living Rudolf Steiner.

After the chapter 'Man and the Evolution of the World' we once again find the path of initiation described, but now in a different way from *'Theosophy'* and *'Knowledge of the Higher Worlds – How Is It Achieved?'* - albeit with the same appeal and the same admonition. This chapter contains the marvellous description of the rose cross meditation.

The conditions for a healthy birth of the higher self are described here once again in a different form; the stages of higher knowledge are described; also the occurrences that await the spiritual pupil - such as, for example, the meeting with the guardian of the threshold – are addressed once more.

The cautious reader, who can hold back his judgments, who can let a judgment *form itself*, will, through the manner in which the author proceeds, experience his full mastership with regard to everything that is described.

Through the development of pure thinking, one finds one's artistic talent

Mystery knowledge does not only provide knowledge – at least when knowledge is not only taken in with the intellect. It also provides for the acquisition of capacities and for changes in personality; one becomes a different, better, more intelligent person, someone who is more competent in life. For this kind of knowledge cannot be acquired without a further development of the skills; on the other hand, it gives back various unexpected possibilities. Thus it is a natural law that the development of pure thinking gives a man a quite different quality. If one wanted to characterize this quality, one could say: one becomes inwardly *romanticized.*

The poet Novalis has expressed this romanticisation as follows:

> 'When I bestow on the common a higher sense,
> On the customary the appearance of mystery,
> On the known the value of the unknown,
> On the temporary the appearance of eternity,
> I romanticize them.'

This romanticizing is actually the artistic interpreting of the world and of life. Pure thinking provides man with this skill and he is thereby released from a dull everyday existence. He does not become a dreamer, but a man who learns to experience the essential in the inessential, the eternal in the temporary. That is by no means easy; he must always rouse himself to the task – but he *has* the capacity for it.

Thus one can understand that Rudolf Steiner, who presents his texts in such logical concepts, had the skill to give art a new impulse in different areas and even create art himself. Thus he initiated Eurythmy and the art of speech formation, but also wrote dramas - mystery dramas that were actually performed on stage and are still performed in anthroposophical circles.

Later, architecture and the arts of painting and sculpture were added to this impulse, through which the Goetheanum in Dornach was built that was to be in itself anthroposophy made visible.

A Bitter Intermezzo

From something that went on purely inwardly, Anthroposophy thus developed into a world of externally visible forms, movements and sounds that were to be the artistic expression of the soul and the spirit. However, this meant that the developing anthroposophy was at the same time exposed to a danger that worked in a really destructive manner over the following decades.

Rudolf Steiner cannot be blamed for that, for he had to do *everything* in his power to bring anthroposophy into the world in such a way that it would also remain present in the world after his death. He gave it shape and development and counted on the fact that the pupils in this development would grow along with it, naturally everyone according to his own ability. Because the artistic reproduction was a fruit of thinking and of initiation built upon that, there should have been some pupils who had at least fully developed pure thinking. Then Rudolf Steiner would not have been the only fundament on which the building Anthroposophy rested; the basis would have been broad and deep enough, because every spiritual participant who contributes pure thinking would enable this basis to grow exponentially. But there was in fact nobody, and Rudolf Steiner said so himself often enough – and when there finally was one (Carl Unger), almost the whole crowd of 'anthroposophers' turned against him.[26]

---

[26] Rudolf Steiner, *Wege und Ziele des geistigen Menschen; Lebensfragen im Lichte der Geisteswissenschaft* (Paths and Aims of the spiritual human being; Life Questions in the Light of Spiritual Science), GA 125, p.76

'You can really feel it in the lectures, which are not esteemed enough, of our dear Dr. Unger, in which you meet with this raising of the human power of knowledge to pure thinking and then in this, the streaming-in of the light of higher worlds. Therefore it must be emphasized: it belongs to the greatest blessings, that we are in the position to have such a force as Dr. Unger in our midst who, in this spiritual-philosophical area, is able to work out of and explain in detail the epistemology of the pure thinking of the subject of knowledge that as the I lies on the level of thinking.'(1910).

And in 1923:[27]

'The scientific concern was until 1919, 1920 more a hope, with the exception of what Dr. Unger fruitfully extracted for anthroposophy from 'The Philosophy of Freedom' and other works of the pre-anthroposophical period. For the rest, aside from what has been built up in this epistemological connection, which was an important content of real substance for the wider movement, we have to say that apart from that, at the beginning of the third period scientific activity was at first but a hope.

And so it was. But we must however bestir ourselves to understand this completely. Gradually, a visible anthroposophy came into being, but the spiritual basis or the spiritual fulfillment was lacking. This was provided exclusively by Rudolf Steiner, while his colleagues amused themselves, despite their meditations and their developing clairvoyance, with the visible externality of eurythmy, dramas etc. Previously, everything had been a completely inward affair that was only handed down via the written and spoken word.

---

[27]   Rudolf Steiner, *Die Geschichte und die Bedingungen der anthroposophischen Bewegung im Verhältnis zur anthroposophischen Gesellschaft* (The History and Conditions of the anthroposophical movement in relation to the Anthroposophical Society), GA 258, p.139

The pupils had at least to become a little active internally in order to grasp it – even when it was evidently taken too lightly. In anthroposophy that has become visible and audible, one easily fell into externalities. To those also belong external rules and standards (no alcohol, no meat, the wearing of specific kinds of clothes, the outward appearance of inner balance etc.).

Whoever wants to form a truthful image of Rudolf Steiner has to want to see this development and concern himself with it, because anthroposophy has become ever more external, while Rudolf Steiner advanced and advances more and more in his spiritual (internal) development – but all alone.

Nevertheless, anthroposophical art has something that goes beyond purely internal spiritual work. The spirit is first found on earth in thinking and knowing with the mind. But it does not live there itself; it casts its shadow over our thoughts. Thoughts are a shadowy form of spirit, but the spirit cannot live in these shadows *itself*. If a free spiritual life is to exist, the spirit must thus free itself from the intellect and learn to experience itself freely. The freedom that can be developed in the intellect abandoned by God can lead to free decisions, but again is actually given up in favour of experiencing the spirit. Pure thinking then transcends itself, and grasps its own spirituality. This spirituality is no longer content, it has as content only that which otherwise escapes the attention as *form*. The spirit can only experience *forms*, not contents. Thus the spirit can only manifest itself as a pure, free spiritual life on earth when it finds pure shapes, in which it can embody itself.

This process which goes on purely within the individual soul, is now externalised as anthroposophical art, especial-

71

ly in eurythmy. The *forms* are externally shaped, externally visible. That is also the case in a less expressive manner in speech formation, theatrical art, in the art of painting, etc., but less purely as form; one has to elaborate the forms more here. In eurythmy form appears on stage *as form*. That is something very special, because on stage something becomes visible – to anyone who can watch – that otherwise can only be experienced in pure thinking that has raised itself to spiritual shape. Certainly, the realm of this inner spiritual form is much, much greater than eurythmic form, because the latter is only a part of the great realm of form. But it actually *becomes* visible for the onlooker.

Seen in this light, it appears that anthroposophical art cannot lose the spirit. And at the time when Marie Steiner was still leading the eurythmy training, the spirit must have been actually experienceable, for she had a *consciousness of form*. This means that not only was form portrayed and shaped but that this portrayal was preceded by a consciousness of the meaning of this form. This form-consciousness must always be present if real anthroposophical art is to arise. The visible ought not to be present as such; it should emerge from a consciousness of form. This consciousness can arise during practice, but practice itself is not yet art.

A eurythmist *must* have within her a consciousness of form. If she does *not* have it, the observer can only see unensouled, spiritless form, and onlookers find this merely repugnant. Spirit can only grasp form and show itself in on earth through form.

By art the spirit can *only be mediated*. Spirit must actually flare up within the individual human being, so that anthroposophy can be carried on in the future. The spirit in art is nevertheless slowly extinguished, because it is not enough when one or two people carry the living spirit inside them. Form must be carried into consciousness over and over again, and then ensouled and spiritualized.

This gradual disappearance of real spirit from anthroposophical art only really started after the death of Rudolf Steiner. Suddenly there was no longer any real spiritual basis, no spiritual fulfillment. Even though this streamed down from the spiritual world, where Rudolf Steiner now was, it could not be experienced outwardly any longer. And because the students had not properly developed themselves inwardly, after the death of Rudolf Steiner anthroposophy lacked a basis and necessary fulfillment. But that is the true nature of decadence: outer glitter but inner emptiness. And anthroposophy immediately fell into decadence and would have fallen apart like a dead body if Rudolf Steiner's followers had not mummified the anthroposophical 'body'. What this means for Rudolf Steiner will be discussed in a later chapter.

Thus since 1925 there has been a mummy, the outer form of which is anthroposophical, but from which all the life has disappeared. Certainly, there are the books and there are the lecture cycles, and because of that, it is still possible to capture something of the living quality of anthroposophy and achieve a living thinking. But this requires a tremendous inner activity, and because our time makes souls ever more passive, people prefer to live only in letters and words, instead of in pure concepts, which are expressed through them. But then one is relating only with the mummy, because the letters and words already died a long time ago. Also, for most people, the volumes of Rudolf Steiner's 'Collected Works' belong to external anthroposophy.

And thus an abomination has developed that is also called

73

'anthroposophy', but which nevertheless works like poison, like everything that is dead. This abomination has been worshipped by whole generations; those that worship it are called 'anthroposophists' and are united in something called the General Anthroposophical Society. They try, each in his own way, to do justice to external anthroposophy. An innumerable number of details have piled up, with which an anthroposophist is supposed to familiarize himself, and by which they test each other. It is a shell that has fallen off, but which still exercises its own effect, even while constantly alienating itself ever further from the original fruit.

If one takes a period of seventy years in which such an abomination can keep on operating in a traditional way, then it will have spent its force around the year 1995. Since then an actual dissolution, a disassociation has been underway. This has become clearly noticeable in the increasing revolt – within the Society – against the founder Rudolf Steiner. In fact the fight is against the mummy, but a lack of the power of discernment has meant that the victim in this fight has become the one who is precisely not responsible for the existence of the mummy, namely, the living Rudolf Steiner.

Meanwhile, there are real 'anthroposophical families', in which the mummy is passed down like an inheritance. There is no escaping it. With Demeter bread one will sooner or later receive quotations from Rudolf Steiner.

Fortunate indeed is the human being who discovers anthroposophy as something 'new', who is not influenced, naïvely, like a member of a different caste, as it were. Indeed, he will never enter the 'chosen' caste – and if he enters it nevertheless, then he also becomes part of the mummy during his life; otherwise, the enthusiastic anthroposopher will remain completely lonely, but he is the one who, un-prejudiced, will have the possibility to come closer to the original being of Rudolf Steiner.

It is in this sense that I write this book – as an apologetic. May it work equally well on both living and dead souls – for any one who wants to know: *who actually was this remarkable man, Rudolf Steiner?*

One can understand that family members of this 'anthro-posophical family', who are raised in it and also perhaps active in it professionally, would like to free themselves from it. But how can one free oneself from a gene? It would mean tearing oneself apart, shaking off the whole pile of rules, with the terrible realization: what then remains?

The branches of the vine have loosened from the original grapevine. They have withered and must be thrown in the fire. But if the grapevine itself is also uprooted and thrown in the fire, then one has really destroyed everything that can help the human race forward. That we nevertheless are standing before this step has become absolutely clear through the appearance of a false prophet such as Judith von Halle; in the Memorandum on the question of Rudolf Steiner's so-called 'racially discriminating statements'[28]; in a book such as 'Missions' by Sebastian Gronbach. Such acts threaten to uproot the grapevine and cast it into the fire.

Wanting to free oneself from a mummy is a justified de-sire. But what is then left over? Because the dead form has remained empty, there is the danger of a void. And the anger one feels about one's own failure and the failure of

---

[28]   Spring 2008

one's predecessors makes one wish to release oneself from the one who gave the original warnings. Away with Rudolf Steiner, away, away! Turn away from him; he belongs to traditional knowledge that is handed down! In the meantime we have come to know so much better, we no longer want to be isolated in the world, we want to be friendly to all other movements...

But what one does not want to recognize as true is that it was the mummy that is isolating, because a healthy, living person does not want to associate with dead bodies. One does want to recognize that the *nothingness* that remains is a void, which fills itself with mockery and hatred, with the being of emptiness of feeling, which we know as Satan or in anthroposophical language - Ahriman.

It is a being that is always present; it does not show itself, but lies within every human being – otherwise he could never die. This being, however, has the power to fill the nothingness with seduction. What happens then if the mummy is destroyed? The filling of the void with Ahriman and the destruction of his arch-enemy - Rudolf Steiner.

We could not spare ourselves this bitter intermezzo. With the externalization of anthroposophy, the destiny of anthroposophy was in a certain way necessarily compromised. 'Necessarily', because anthroposophy had to externalize itself; 'compromised', because there had not been sufficient inner development among the followers of Rudolf Steiner.

*

Now we shall turn to the living grapevine and try further to understand how Rudolf Steiner worked as spiritual scientist.

He was an independent spiritual scientist, who proffered his fully christianised occult science as a spiritual Communion. But of course, in doing so, he also called forth resistance within the Theosophical Society. Thus his insights that Christ is the absolute centre of the development of man and earth, and that the mystery of Golgotha was absolutely unique, were opposed by the election of a new 'Christ' (the boy Krishnamurti). As theosopher, Rudolf Steiner was actually supposed to teach that this boy was the reincarnated Christ. But he responded with a lecture cycle on the four gospels, produced a fifth gospel, which he had 'read' through spiritual research in the Akashic Chronicle, and remained faithful to his insights up to the final consequence of his actions: exclusion from the Theosophical Society and the foundation of the Anthroposophical Society (1912/1913). I mention this here as an historical event; in the next chapter I shall go into the meaning of the christological lectures. This all runs in parallel with the beginning of his artistic activity.

Rudolf Steiner wrote four plays, in which anthroposophy appears once more profoundly, in images of the development of several characters and the representation of spritual beings who work with or against that development. Due to their great expressive strength, the plays were written in half-poetic form, spoken in very expressive speech (in order to allow the original working of the word be more experienced more strongly) and the action was interwoven by moving eurythmists. One actually sees – when one wants to open up to it – a spiritual world on stage; one sees how different spiritual beings work and how people are connected to each other by Karma (destiny), often confounded in a knot.

Great theatrical performances were produced; but

now, after about a century, the mummy-nature works so strongly that only with the utmost inner exertion can one imagine how it must have been originally. Just as a performance of Bach's St. Matthew Passion in our time is in danger of becoming spiritless, a performance of the Mystery Dramas also withdraws from its original life force.

In the forming of artistic speech Rudolf Steiner wanted speech to become audible as an expression of the holy word. That caused the reciter to speak vowels and consonants in a very expressive manner, each sound according to its own being. For the sober people of our time it is hard to listen to. One may have a certain fear of such expressive speech, because it does not sound 'normally' human. But one has to speak to oneself and try to understand how the spiritual in life is being entirely eliminated, how this occurs through a levelling out, a making things plain and simple; they cannot be normal and simple enough these days. The levelled-out, simple human being gets goose bumps when he has to listen to 'anthroposophical' artistic speech. This is reinforced by the disappearance of *life*. Only when one wants to move in an unprejudiced way through such a spoken language in spite of everything can one experience something of its original greatness.

Eurythmy externalizes anthroposophy even further. On the stage the being of vowels and consonants is made visible, how they make the speech organs move and what actually comes to expression in the deeper sense. A description of eurythmy is actually impossible; one has to see and experience it, then it immediately becomes clear what it is. Alongside it, there is tone-eurythmy, in which not speech but music is made visible.

I shall be accused of including this form of art with the

mummy, but there are nevertheless living and *capable* artists, who still express this art. That actually applies to the whole of anthroposophy: everything that it has brought forward in the way of human achievement since 1925 is something living, is it not? Have not countless well-meaning and willing people exerted themselves? I do not want to say anything against particular individuals. I also do not wish to maintain that a living anthroposophy is impossible without a Rudolf Steiner present on earth. The only thing that I maintain here is that the attempt to 'spiritualize' the visible anthroposophical building, the whole of anthroposophy, from the inside out, to fill it with pure spirit has not been successful. Even if a eurythmist does her work enthusiastically and capably, even if the leader of a eurythmy group is a great artist with great understanding – these things do not make a performance anthroposophical. There should be people who have developed an inwardly empowered pure thinking; only through this could a free spiritual life and an anthroposophical *movement* exist that could resurrect the entire form and being of anthroposophy on earth. Such people would not even need to be this eurythmist or that eurythmy group leader. There should be capable spiritual scientists to whom the eurythmist and the group leader could go for advice.

The fact that in anthroposophical art, which ought to be *alive*, exactly the spirit is missing – because there is no-one who carries that spirit as movement inside himself - makes this art repel normal people, instead of motivating and uplifting them, as Rudolf Steiner hoped it would. Anthroposophers themselves can still do something with modern eurythmy, because they stand strongly together, because they work on each other, and everything is in good order. But eurythmy was not meant to be performed only for anthroposophers. It was supposed to conquer the world. But the world *is* already spiritless; it cannot bear to be shown dead images of the spirit. Eurythmy does not give spectators the shudders because they are afraid of the spirit, but because of their fear of spiritlessness. That is something that the anthroposophical leadership should take seriously!

The Christian lectures of Rudolf Steiner

After 'Christianity as Mystical Fact' Rudolf Steiner did not
write any other book about anthroposophical Christianity
or about Christian anthroposophy. He only gave lectures.
The lecturer thus always had a certain group of people in
front of him, he was not – as with writing a book – direct-
ing himself to the whole world. Only the small book 'The
Spiritual Guidance of the Individual and Humanity'[29] re-
states something from the lectures.

In the Christian lectures, however, one gets to know Rudolf Steiner in his deep Christian nature. The stenographed
texts that more or less literally reproduce the lectures, show
the sensitive reader how the heart of Rudolf Steiner became
profound and grateful, how thoroughly the pious thoughts
were formed, how he lovingly gave himself to this or that
being. This way of speaking should make even more of an
impression than the content and the texts (that already
work astonishingly upon one). In the sentences one can still
witness how the knowing spirit and soul of Rudolf Steiner
could change according to what he was speaking about.
Thus the whole mood of the lectures about the Luke Gospel
steeped in the love and compassion that are developed in
Buddhism. The healing power of this love, this compassion,
lives in every phrase. Once one has experienced that profoundly, one could never say - as, for example, do Sebastian
Gronbach *et al.*[30] - that Rudolf Steiner only used Christ as

---

[29]   Rudolf Steiner, *Die geistige Führung des Menschen und der Menschheit*,
       GA 15 (The Spiritual Leadership of Man and of Mankind)

[30]   See n.23

an image to express something totally different.

In the early Christian book ('Christianity as Mystical Fact') this affection is not yet present in this way, but in the spoken word it can be deeply experienced from approximately 1907 onwards. When one lives into the spiritual melodies of Novalis, one dives into the Christ-experience. When one reads the Christian lectures of Rudolf Steiner, the experience goes even further because one receives unprecedented Christian wisdom, *insights* that satisfy every soul that longs for Christ deeply, as well as changes in one's feelings that lead directly to the Christ-*experience*. When the reader only tries intensely to let his mind's judgement move along with what is being said, and experience, as it were, musically in his soul, what there is to be experienced, he not only expands his insights, but above all fills his heart with the real Christ being. Rudolf Steiner was not only a gifted teacher, he was an initiate and capable of making the spiritual world become tangible. In reality, each lecture must have been a soul-stirring happening – because even in the cool form of written text this happening can still be felt and taken into one's own soul.

Could a man, who was so steeped in Christ that it can even be experienced in his transcribed lectures ever make the unchristian statements of which he is now accused? Naturally, if Christ had not have existed, if this love and this compassion had not proceeded from a divine being on earth, then Rudolf Steiner could by chance have made the kind of unfeeling and discriminating statements[31] that every other human being makes, which is what is now ima-

---

[31]   In 2008 the 'racism issue' against Rudolf Steiner was very virulent.

gined of him.[32]

It requires thinking that is profound, differentiated, and dynamic in order to be able to comprehend the true meaning of these statements. When one tears several paragraphs from their context and judges them with crude reasoning, one does not grasp the meaning of them. One connects to words concepts that one possesses oneself without asking oneself explicitly what all this *actually means*, without applying hypersensitive, trendy or populist ideas as the only judge. When a twenty year-old boy has *one* grey hair and one pulls it out and gives it to someone else and asks him for the age of this person, he will think that it is from a greybeard. But one does exactly the same when one wants to judge isolated statements torn from their context. That non-anthroposophers get agitated about these isolated statements is simply understandable. But that people who know the value of the work of Rudolf Steiner can behave in such a 'foolish' manner is absolutely incomprehensible.

To them, the loving, compassionate nature of the founder of anthroposophy should be a fact that they can still experience. And thus these statements, which disturb one, should be seen in the light of the whole as much as possible, in order to tell the people who are unable to understand so deeply what was actually meant there. For one *can* truly understand every statement and show that what was spoken was spoken out of love for humanity. One can explain that the individual should never think that it is about him, because it was not meant that way. But whoever finally wants to free himself from this 'all-knowing' Rudolf Steiner, thankfully seizes the stick with which he can finally

---

[32] See the 'Memorandum' written by Ramon Brüll and Jens Heisterkamp about the alleged discriminating statements made by Rudolf Steiner.

slay him, or even better, he enables others to seize the stick and deal with the matter. The technique is already ancient; it was already known in the days of Elijah the prophet:[33]

So she wrote letters in Ahab's name, and sealed them with his seal, and sent the letters unto the elders and to the nobles that were in his city, dwelling with Naboth. And she wrote in the letters, saying, Proclaim a fast, and set Naboth on high among the people: And set two men, sons of Belial, before him, to bear witness against him, saying, Thou didst blaspheme God and the king. And then carry him out, and stone him, that he may die.

And the men of his city, even the elders and the nobles who were the inhabitants in his city, did as Jezebel had sent unto them, and as it was written in the letters which she had sent unto them. They proclaimed a fast, and set Naboth on high among the people. And there came in two men, children of Belial, and sat before him: and the men of Belial witnessed against him, even against Naboth, in the presence of the people, saying, Naboth did blaspheme God and the king. Then they carried him forth out of the city, and stoned him with stones, that he died. Then they sent to Jezebel, saying, Naboth is stoned, and is dead.

And it came to pass, when Jezebel heard that Naboth was stoned, and was dead, that Jezebel said to Ahab, Arise, take possession of the vineyard of Naboth the Jezreelite, which he refused to give thee for money: for Naboth is not alive, but dead. And it came to pass, when Ahab heard that Naboth was dead, that Ahab rose up to go down to the vineyard of Naboth the Jezreelite, to take possession of it.

And the word of the LORD came to Elijah the Tishbite, saying, Arise, go down to meet Ahab king of Israel, which is in Samaria: behold, he is in the vineyard of Naboth, whither he is gone down to possess it. And thou shalt speak unto him, saying, Thus saith the LORD, Hast thou killed, and also taken possession? And thou shalt

---

[33]   The Old Testament, Luther's translation 1912, I Kings 21:8-21,24

speak unto him, saying, Thus saith the LORD, In the place where
dogs licked the blood of Naboth shall dogs lick thy blood, even thine.
And Ahab said to Elijah, Hast thou found me, O mine enemy? And
he answered, I have found thee: because thou hast sold thyself to
work evil in the sight of the LORD. Behold, I will bring evil upon
thee, and will take away thy posterity, and will cut off from Ahab
him that pisseth against the wall, and him that is shut up and left
in Israel, And will make thine house like the house of Jeroboam the
son of Nebat, and like the house of Baasha the son of Ahijah, for the
provocation wherewith thou hast provoked me to anger, and made
Israel to sin.And of Jezebel also spake the LORD, saying, The dogs
shall eat Jezebel by the wall of Jezreel. Him that dieth of Ahab in
the city the dogs shall eat; and him that dieth in the field shall the
fowls of the air eat. (1 Kings 21, 8-14)

Rudolf Steiner during the First World War

In the years 1914-1918 anthroposophy, as it were, withdraws into itself again. There are almost no esoteric meetings, performances of the Mystery dramas stop, and the planned fifth play is not written. Work is mainly dedicated to the construction of the Goetheanum. In his lectures Rudolf Steiner also always commemorates those who have fallen on the battlefield, and with regard to the content he reacts deeply to the mystery of death. Two books are published that indicate how a new internalization of anthroposophy takes place.

'Riddles of the Soul'[34] shows a clear exposition of the threefold nature of the human body and its cohesion with the human soul. Also, the path of spiritual development is briefly described in a new way as proceeding from natural scientific thinking. One can feel how here again the link is made to his early epistemological writings. While in the intervening period the connection was mostly made with Theosophy and the purely Christian form of spiritual science was developed as anthroposophy, now Theosophy works on only on the background, in its fruits. Inner development, linked onto the 'Philosophy of Freedom', comes forward in a deeply touching way once more in 'The Riddle of Man'.

While in time of war not a lot can be done outwardly, the primal impulse of anthroposophy emerges once again with all its force and dignity. What Rudolf Steiner described in

---

[34]   Rudolf Steiner, *Riddles of the Soul*, GA 21

'The Course Of My Life', in which he accentuated the development of the will aspect of his cognition, which culminated in the meeting with Christ, is clearly expressed in the chapter 'Future Prospects' in 'The Riddle of Humanity', so that it becomes understandable how one can follow this path oneself. If this original impulse could have been the fundament and spiritual fulfilment for anthroposophy and had been taken up by the members, the lifeless externalization would never have been able to arise that nowadays threatens to end up in dissociating the members from each other. I shall quote a part of this chapter, to point in Steiner's own words to the essence of anthroposophical work:[35]

> *Now such an awakening is altogether possible, however, through one's developing, in inner (soul) experience, a certain activation differing from the usual — of the powers of one's soul being (thought and will experiences). The indication that with the idea of the awakened consciousness one is continuing in the direction taken by Goethe's world view can show that our study here wishes to have nothing to do with the mental pictures of any muddled mysticism. Through an inner strengthening, one can lift oneself out of the state of ordinary consciousness and in doing so experience something similar to the transition from dreaming into wakeful mental picturing. Whoever passes from dreaming into a waking state experiences how will penetrates into the course of his mental pictures, whereas in dreaming he is given over to the course of his dream pictures without his own will involvement. What occurs through unconscious processes when one awakens from sleep can be effected on a different level by conscious soul activity. The human being can bring a stronger exercise of will into his ordinary conscious thinking than is present there in his usual experience of the physical world. Through this he can pass over from thinking to an experience of*

---

35   Steiner, *The Riddle of Man*, GA 20, p. 160ff

thinking. In ordinary consciousness, thinking is not experienced; rather, through thinking, one experiences what is thought. But there is an inner work the soul can do that gradually brings one to the point of living, not in what is thought, but rather in the very activity of thinking itself. A thought that is not simply received from the ordinary course of life but rather is placed into one's consciousness with will in order that one experience it in its thought nature: such a thought releases different forces in the soul than one that is evoked by the presence of outer impressions or by the ordinary course of one's soul life. And when, ever anew within itself, the soul rouses that devotion — practiced only to a small degree, in fact, in ordinary life — to thoughts as such, when the soul concentrates upon thoughts as thoughts: then it discovers within itself powers that are not employed in ordinary life but remain slumbering (latent), as it were. These are powers that are discovered only through conscious use. But they predispose the soul to an experience not present before their discovery. The thoughts fill themselves with a life all their own, which the thinking (meditating) person feels to be connected with his own soul being. (What is meant here by "seeing consciousness" does not arise from ordinary waking consciousness through bodily [physiological] processes the way ordinary waking consciousness arises from dream consciousness. In the awakening from this latter consciousness into day consciousness, one has to do with a changing engagement [Einstellung] of the body relative to outer reality. In the awakening from ordinary consciousness into seeing consciousness, one has to do with a changing engagement of one's soul-spiritual way of picturing things relative to a spiritual world.)

For this discovery of the life in thoughts, however, the expenditure of conscious will is necessary. But this cannot simply be that will which appears in ordinary consciousness. The will must also become engaged in a different way and in a different direction, so to speak, than for experience in mere sense-perceptible existence. In ordinary life one feels oneself to be at the center of what one wills or what one wants. For even in wanting, a kind of held-back will is at work.

The will streams out from the "I" and down into desire, into bodily movement, into one's action. A will in this direction is ineffective for the soul's awakening out of ordinary consciousness. But there is also a direction of will that in a certain sense is the opposite of this. It is at work when, without any direct look at an outer result, a person seeks to direct his own "I". This direction of the will manifests in a person's efforts to shape his thinking into something meaningful and to improve upon his feelings, and in all his impulses of self-education. In a gradual intensification of the will forces present in a person in this direction there lies what he needs in order to awaken out of his ordinary consciousness.

It becomes clear, in which way the philosopher has become spiritual scientist through Christianity. One can see the series of incarnations more or less in this development: the philosopher, the religious, saintly philosopher, the spiritual scientist – with few externally known incarnations in-between these. It is not possible – because it contradicts every logical justification - to acknowledge the fullness of an individuality in all its incarnations and then throw away some of its fruits as worthless, poisonous or rotten. When one has acknowledged the fruits of a personality as *good*, these indicate the goodness of this personality. The same applies the other way round: when one has got to know the personality, one can not simply declare his fruits to be worthless. However, this does happen in our time, because logical thinking is only applied to ultra-short stretches of time. When a line of thought is a little longer or when it includes the unpredictable, the non-measurable, then logical thinking lets go, and in its place steps personal feeling, taste etc.

In Europe chaos rules. Chaos can be used for something
positive when it becomes a ground for fertilization. Political and Social life is overwhelmed; socialism and commu-
nism gain the upper hand.

Rudolf Steiner outlines his spiritual impulse and comes
forward with a new idea: the threefolding of the social organism. He has already elaborated threefolding for the human being in his book 'Riddles of the Soul'; now it is placed
at the basis of the reformation of social and political life.
The idea connects to the slogan of the French revolution:
Freedom, Equality and Brotherhood. The ingenuity of this
idea is that it does not apply in the same way to all layers
of social life. Freedom is the sign of spiritual life, equality
the sign of the life of rights, and brotherhood rules in economic life. That is the ideal. Everywhere lectures are given,
especially also for socialistically-inclined workers. Enthusiasm arises for the idea, but the organisers of lectures have
very different motives. Rudolf Steiner is mainly criticised
for his idealism. It is not believed possible that the modern human being, who has become so strongly egotistical,
could live in such an altruistically conceived society.

The spiritual approach of Rudolf Steiner comes very
clearly to the fore here. The 'practical' man wants to shape
social and political life *so* that it is 'realistic'. One judges
according to what happens to be present and what one
can expect, because that is held to be 'practical'. But the
ideas of a spiritual scientist like Rudolf Steiner do not come
'from the earth'; they come from 'above', from the spiritual
world, conceived through love for the earth. People living

on the earth should try to take in these ideas with a logical mind, and with them, enthuse their feelings and stir up their will. Then the idea shapes social relations on earth; it is not created from earthly relations. Rudolf Steiner wanted to presume that his contemporaries were equal to this test. Naturally, he did not expect a perfect realization of the idea, but he knew that the idea was formed in accordance with spiritual and earthly reality and that it was really powerful; it had the power really to change the situation on earth.

The threefolding of the social organism could not be realized, in spite of all the efforts of Rudolf Steiner and his co-workers. Nowadays, one is not even expected to try to realize it. If there is *something* that has changed tremendously, it is the social and political life and the human being that is more or less undergoing this change. The three spheres – spiritual life, rights life and economic life – have become much more intertwined than in Rudolf Steiner's time; they are now more or less inseparable. The economic sphere rules the state, and the state rules spiritual life. Actually, business has the power. It could not have been otherwise, because only strong spiritual powers can bring about a free spiritual life, and this strength has not been developed at all – that was the task for anthroposophers. A spiritual scientist should have emerged who could put forward the idea and the design in a form that fits the times. Not with crude intellect or by using traditional ideas, even if these had come originally from Rudolf Steiner. Here it is really the case that the ideas of Rudolf Steiner cannot simply be transferred to the current time. The disease of the present spiritual life – if such a life exists at all – lies in the lack of inner experience. A eurythmy student learns to experience the vowels and the consonants mostly when he experiences the gestures that belong to it. But that is an experiencing of something external, even if the external gesture is an expression of the spiritual. The accent in learning eurhythmy should be on experiencing the vowels and consonants internally, and on experiencing how such a feeling comes to expression in an external gesture. Only that would be a real eurythmising, when through internal experiencing, this experience *itself* would become externally visible. I have called this a realization, a consciousness, of the form.

Thus it is with everything in anthroposophy, whether it is philosophy, religion, art, science or the social questions. Inner experience should manifest itself externally. However, this internal experience should be expressed with the strongest spiritual force, otherwise there is absolutely nothing that can come to expression.

When the external, however, becomes a starting point for design (even if this external is called 'anthroposophy') one draws one's behaviour into the sickness of the present time. In ordinary life there are already enough possibilities to experience and enjoy what is external. In anthroposophy, the movement must be completely reversed – otherwise there *is* no movement, and one only sees a dead Rudolf Steiner.

The art of the Goetheanum

During wartime the Goetheanum is built on the Dornach Hill. Rudolf Steiner is the architect; the decoration, also the paintings and statues, the frescoes, the paintings on the windows, everything happens under his direction. Anthroposophy, occult science, is to become a visible sheath for the anthroposophical work.

In the centre of this building a statue is to be placed, a great figure, that is to represent *man*. The figure of Man, how he has to maintain himself between polarities, is sculpted – from wood. Man, who succeeds in keeping Lucifer and Ahriman (the Devil and Satan respectively) in balance, becomes similar to Christ. This representative of Man can thus be experienced as an image of Christ. The English sculptor Edith Maryon has the skill, to sculpt this statue from wood. Rudolf Steiner carries the idea, the image, the figure, the meaning in his spirit, and through the hands of Edith Maryon – though he too, often works on the sculpture – the figure appears in wood.

Through this statue one can experience the Christian nature of anthroposophy. Not a few people are repelled by the statue. One imagines something sweeter, something more amiable, not this powerful, earnest strength, this determined gesture, these terrible images around the man and also behind him. Nevertheless, one finds in experiencing it true anthroposophy here, and when one can maintain an unprejudiced attitude, the appearance of the Christ figure makes a deep impression on one's experience. Then one feels *also* this man once again, the philosopher, the philosopher-saint, the spiritual scientist, the transformer of the world. One feels *the living Rudolf Steiner, for whom the name is much too small...*

Anthroposophy on its path into life

Rudolf Steiner is more and more engaged in carrying through spiritual science in the sciences and in life after the war. Much is asked of him, and these questions call forth great insights. Much of what the non-anthroposopher associates with anthroposophy derives from this time.

An anthroposophical medical science comes into being, biodynamic farming, a broadening of natural science, a Waldorf school pedagogy. A movement for religious renewal begins - the Christian Community. All the co-workers in these various fields ask Rudolf Steiner for courses, lectures, directions and manuals. The membership grows and becomes international. Anthroposophy becomes something to be reckoned with.

The opposition, however, also grows and cumulates in a violent attack: the Goethanum burns down almost completely (New Years Eve 1922/23). The sculpture of Christ remains undamaged because it was not yet in its place in the Goetheanum.

There is a description of this night in the book about Marie Steiner by Marie Savitch. The description is startling. One experiences a deep tragedy, the absolute powerlessness of Rudolf Steiner and his friends, who do everything that can be done to put out the fire – yet the fire flares up higher and higher and everybody knows that the Goetheanum is hopelessly lost. I quote from another witness, who wrote down her memories of the event in her notebook in 1935:[36]

'You saw Dr. Steiner everywhere then; he was soon on the site, which he crossed in all directions, then he was in the carpentry workshop (Schreinerei), always with a deeply sad and earnest expression without excitement, fully aware of what was being lost for mankind in the destruction of this work. The building was unique and carried the entire development of the world and of mankind in its forms and images. To be inside this building meant, for every person sensitive to it, a stirring of the deepest grounds of his creating power.

Because of its forms both internal and external, because of its frescoes and ceiling paintings, its window paintings, and its columns that were made of different kinds of wood, with such meaningful sculptures on the capitals, this building was a landmark for man, above all for those who could understand what they were looking at.

In the building the signs of the secrets of the past, present and future were hidden, but nevertheless public, because everyone could see them. That is why it is an unforgettable experience for those souls who had the good fortune to be able to spend time in the building. In one night the long work of ten years had been destroyed. Dr. Steiner stood before the ruins of the building once more at eight o'clock in the morning; it was still burning and smoking. Most people went home, the site was empty, while faithful souls cleared out the atelier, and prepared the carpentry workshop once more for work.
Alone he stood there and endured the destruction. I dared to come close to him with humility and could only say the words: 'It is terrible for us'. 'Yes, he said, 'now everything is inscribed in the world ether.' (Notebook 74)

---

[36] E. Zeylmans van Emmichhoven, *Wer war Ita Wegman?* (Who Was Ita Wegman?), Vol. 1

To Count Polzer-Hoditz Rudolf Steiner said the next day:[32]

'The differentiation of the souls is too great. They do want to see and hear everything, and to be present everywhere, but they do not want to wake up. Thus they have to awaken through catastrophes and personal pain. It is not karma that is at work here, but only the lack of wakefulness of the members and the human jealousy that extends right into the physical. The possibility was given to have the space of the Word among us, but the space of the Word can only exist, when it has its resemblance, its lively image in the heart, in the conscientiousness of the Word, which means, when man does not only listen, but also can and wants to carry responsibility, like a person responsible for himself before the 'Word of the world'. That was the sense of the building: Word and answer. Logos and man.

In Ephesus we had the incarnation secret of the Word before us. It had to be destroyed, because otherwise the counter-forces could have unfolded an important centre of their activities there, for the jealousy of the gods was active up in the atmosphere. Here, however, there is a reversal. The gods looked to the space of the Word expectantly, but man was not there to protect the building. A possibility was given, but the answer of man failed to appear; only jealousy was not silent.'

(from an unpublished diary of Ludwig van Polzer-Hoditz)

But the next day, lectures went on as normal. What a man, who could achieve such a thing! His visible life's work lies completely in ashes – and he goes on with his work with even greater power.

In 1923, however, Rudolf Steiner blamed his students,

co-workers and followers for a great deal.[37] He states directly that this blow of fate, the arson attack, could never have
been successful if the members had lived with anthroposophy in a different way. There was a lack of inner activity;
a lack of seriousness in acknowledging the enthusiasm of
opponents; a sectarian tendency in the Society, the forming
of cliques, a sort of a family that does not let outsiders in;
no interest in what is actually going on in the world ... etc.

It was not possible to work on further like this. A choice
had to be made: either Rudolf Steiner withdraws from the
Society with several of his most faithful followers and forms
an Order; or he disbands the Society and founds a new one
and becomes president of it (until then Rudolf Steiner was
not even a member of the Society because he thought he
should not do that as a spiritual scientist).

The second course is taken. The foundation of the new
Society takes place during the 'Christmas Conference'
1923/24.

'We all know that!' an anthroposopher might exclaim at
this point. That may be, but it must no longer be a matter of simple familiarity with these facts. The knowing of
them is to be refreshed, so that it is present again in one's
consciousness. However, it is now a matter of *experiencing*
this extensive knowing as profoundly as possible, as if the
knowledge were completely new. Only then we can hope
to gain an idea of the being of this great Master of the Occident. Let us experience deeply how he sought to permeate
life on earth in its varied forms with his full, immense spiritual power. He shows us an unstoppable activity, the like of

---

[37]   *Das Schicksalsjahr 1923* (The Year of Destiny 1923), GA 259

which one can hardly conceive. After the philosopher had tried to grasp the appearances of the world with thinking, now the spiritual scientist strove to carry his knowledge over into the world. And he had to fight against unbelievable obstacles that came from this world, and which were put in his way. The understanding of the members was a shortcoming, something that was missing. In the external becomes visible, what the spiritual scientist has already created inside himself long before: an unbelievable, never weakening activity that even begins there where all natural power is exhausted.

There are 'anthroposophers', who think that one can exceed Rudolf Steiner by simply sitting behind a computer[38] in order to achieve a blissful all-in-one experience. The serious human being should form an image of that and put against it the image of Rudolf Steiner's activity described above. That is why we are *human*, in order to experience these differences and learn to sense the truth in them.

---

[38] See n.23

The Christmas Conference 1923/1924

With the Christmas Conference we see once more an immense internalization occurring. However, a great outward Society is founded, something that could look like an externalization. But a basis is made, the basis for the new Goetheanum. However, this was not to be accomplished externally – although it is constructed externally again – but in the hearts of the members. It is a very clear call for inner development that the members receive in this foundation, in the form of a meditation.

There exist all kind of speculations about the Christmas Conference and what happened after it. But one thing is absolutely clear: because Rudolf Steiner had taken on the leadership of the Society, he was now connected to it. That was realized through the influx of an 'esoteric impulse' throughout the Society. If the Society had 'only' been an external organization before, now it was itself an esoteric one. Living anthroposophy, like it lived inside Rudolf Steiner, flowed directly through the Society, because he took on the leadership of it.

One cannot therefore interpret that as purely an external measure, but as a magical act, an initiation of the Society. This had to show itself worthy of the initiation in what followed. Was it up to it, or not? One cannot come to a different conclusion than: it was *not*. When the spirit connects to the body and is 'embodied', the body has to give itself to that. But if it resists too much, the spirit has to withdraw. How else could one explain the complete breakdown of the physical powers of Rudolf Steiner on the 24th of September 1924, than that he was called back by the spiritual world or that he returned to it himself? With any other human being one could say, he just happens to be overloaded, overtired, exhausted. Although Rudolf Stei-ner in announcements gave this exhaustion as the reason for the postponement of his work, one has to look at this much more spiritually, which he himself *also* indicated very clearly. One can only make judgments about the true state of affairs when one looks at all the reports together. In the Society there was much speculation about Rudolf Steiner being ill in those days. Mainly, there was talk about the consequences of a poisoning at a 'Rout' (a reception) on the 1st of January 1924.[39] Rudolf Steiner published a statement that was supposed to silence such talk.[40] In it he clearly states that his forces were failing because of the demands from the members that resulted from his enormous lecturing activity. As to the latter, he said that '*I could manage all that quite well, I did not have to be scared that my forces would fail...*' He saw this as fate and as something that would pass. That was the official declaration. From medical science we know that the hope for healing may never be given up – it truly ends only at death. But there was another side to the official declaration, a more spiritual one. And one has to want to look back at that. Rudolf Steiner had performed an initiation during the Christmas Conference, and that would have required from him all the forces necessary – if the Society had only devoted itself.

The exhaustion of his powers proves that the Society, the members, had not passed the test. They proceeded too much as usual, did not take the situation seriously enough, underestimated it. The 'anthroposophical movement', the

---

[39] I worked this out in *'Rudolf Steiner, eine spirituelle Biographie'*, 2011

[40] See GA 260a, Documents 1924/1925, p.40

'esoteric direction', remained with Rudolf Steiner, the pupils did not take it on from him, did not make themselves ready for the communion with the spirit. These are no assumptions. An intensive living-into the facts gives one the logical justification and the inescapable proof for this course of events. It could not at all be otherwise. After the 24th September there was one possibility for improvement left: Rudolf Steiner himself maintains the strong hope that he will become healthy again. But it does not depend on him anymore. His great spiritual power is given to the Society; he is no longer able to heal himself. It depends on the acts, on the attitude of the members of the Society. That was still insufficiently understood. His greatness was insufficiently perceived, and *therefore* he was not understood. *This* was particularly emphasised with reproach by his wife Marie Steiner–von Sivers after his death: his greatness had not been recognised! He who does not understand his own spirit, pushes it away and it must withdraw. Rudolf Steiner had to withdraw and he died on 30th March 1925. And with that, Anthroposophy also died; it became a dead thing. The Anthroposophical Society became a corpse.

If anthroposophers today would only have the modesty to think this through thoroughly, see it and experience it. Then they would firmly act on behalf of Rudolf Steiner, when he is accused wrongfully, because he cannot defend himself. Then it would not have been necessary to look for friends in other spiritual streams; these would become partly redundant, because those who search for true spirituality would find it in anthroposophy – instead of being repelled by it and having to join with less productive paths.

Now the stubborn view persists that the Anthroposophical Society founded at the Christmas Conference still has the same connection to its founder as in 1924. It is stated that Rudolf Steiner has connected his karma to the karma of the Society and that consequently, the anthroposopher must feel obliged to sacrifice himself for this Society and remain faithful to it out of love for Rudolf Steiner – whatever the future may bring.

In the next chapter I shall attempt to bring some clarity to this question and its answer.

The karma of Rudolf Steiner in relation to the karma of the Anthroposophical Society

In relation to anthroposophy I belong to the (many) 'displaced souls', souls that can not find their home in the General Anthroposophical Society, even if they have been members of it for years, or still are. One who loves the spiritual scientist Rudolf Steiner as spiritual teacher, who loves anthroposophy, seeks for a home in the General Anthroposophical Society, on the one hand out of an awful homesickness for an anthroposophy realized on earth, but on the other hand out of an intense desire to be able to work on this realization himself. There are anthroposophers who feel at home within 'the broad church' of the Society and who can enjoy the 'family feeling' of the soul of the group. Others feel less comfortable there, but can still remain faithful to the Society because they experience something familiar somewhere.

I myself have never been able to feel that way. Of course I know the objection that will immediately be made: 'that is not us, but yourself!' Or: 'we understand what you mean, but you have to remain faithful to the association, because Rudolf Steiner has connected to it, he has connected his karma to the karma of the General Anthroposophical Society that was founded at the Christmas Conference. Because this is such a forceful statement, I must go into it a bit deeper.

First, I want to elaborate on the fact that someone who knows herself to be as united with anthroposophy as I am, still feels a 'displaced soul'. Later, I shall conduct a spiritual examination of this constantly occurring allegation that Rudolf Steiner is still, as it were, one with the General

Anthroposophical Society.

What constantly brings about this displaced feeling? I have always strongly lived from the spirit, also in times when I was completely unaware of it. Pure thinking was for me a strong need in all life situations, also before my 'anthroposophical period'. Subsequently, anthroposophical truths came before my spirit, before my soul, in their pure forms, and I could not do other than experience them, as it were, as forms of the spiritual researcher himself: expressions of his being, through which spiritual beings could make themselves known. I have never been able to experience anthroposophical sentences other than that they belonged to the spiritual scientist himself. In other words: thinker and thought were for me one and the same. It was not that Rudolf Steiner did not express *more* than his own being, for he did that excellently. But he did not live separately from his words, from his thoughts. He was one with them. All other writers and speakers speak 'about' something. Not Rudolf Steiner; he empathizes – and within him, the spiritual world – in his words. He does not pour himself into them, but is truly one and the same with them. If one reads a line, one takes in the man himself, together with the content that is read.

But then one enters a room where a member's meeting is to take place, where a lecture is being given. The words that are spoken are similar, but the spiritually experiencing soul is torn, because the soul longs for the spiritual part of these words, but only finds deadliness. Everything is dead; spirit and soul have withdrawn from it. The people who are present do have soul and spirit, but they speak dead words. Why are they dead? Because they are empty shells, these words. They can still be understood, and the understanding of them is still available. But the spirit is not present, that belongs in them, that should be in them, that had to be in them. Which spirit is not there? The spirit that can still be found immediately with a pure thinking in the books and lectures of Rudolf Steiner – it is completely lacking as soon as anthroposophy is spoken, lectured on or written about: the spirit of the spiritual scientist himself is missing. Thus if, with a spiritually experiencing soul, one attends a meeting of anthroposophers, the soul is torn. The trusted word, that can simply be *so* lively, has died, is dead, dead, dead. The soul encounters something that has completely loosened itself from the original spirit and has its own lifeless existence. Other spiritual beings can pull it towards them somewhat; the whole anthroposophical heritage drifts further and further away from the original spirit and takes on a terribly deformed shape.

Why are there then so many satisfied members in the General Anthroposophical Society? Because they take in everything abstractly, because their own spirit is not participating at all.[41] Because they do not develop pure thinking, they do not want to develop pure thinking at all, and because of that, they are not present with their own will, which is a spiritual fact – because the will is spirit. There is then only a collection of heads in the room, who experience all kinds of personal things in what the head thinks. The spirit is not present. The thoughts are ruled instead of being fully and totally impregnated with the will. It is like a puppet theatre of thoughts, in which the player has the arrogance to put himself above the puppets (thoughts), instead of entering into it, like a performer does. The spirit of Rudolf Steiner is not present. If one wants to experience

---

[41] Nobody should be offended by this. For I speak generally, not personally. It is the 'general being', that is discussed here, never the individual being. The 'general being' overrules the individual, or the individual suffers.

the spirit, one can only die in this Society.

If someone approaches you and says: 'You must remain a member, because Rudolf Steiner has connected himself to the Society'- that misses the point completely, because the deeply experiencing soul is torn precisely because of the *absence of this spirit.* From the first day on, this was clear to me; however, I could not understand it myself yet. I could only suffer something that I thought to be legitimate, without exactly knowing what the cause of the suffering was. Over the years, the cause has become consciously clear to me. Nevertheless, I remained a member, because I always wanted to doubt this insight. Only because of the position adopted by the Executive Council (Vorstand) in the question of racism or discrimination in the work of Rudolf Steiner in 1998 in the Netherlands did the last thread that still remained between the Society and Rudolf Steiner snap: this thread was trust in the Master.

Through the above-mentioned experiences it becomes clear that Rudolf Steiner is not connected to the General Anthroposophical Society; he is not present. Words are present, but real thoughts no longer are.

With the 'Christmas Conference' of 1923/1924 Rudolf Steiner refounded the Society, took on the chairmanship himself and caused his spirit with its esoteric insights to flow through the Society. With that he certainly took a step which works on karmically. The idea, however, that in doing so, he connected himself 'forever' with the fate of the General Anthroposophical Society is a statement without foundation, and disguises the true facts of the matter. It works as a dogma, because if one adapts one's life in accordance with a statement that one cannot penetrate fully, one obeys a dogma.

Now I am fully aware that, with this thought, I am here touching on a theme that is deeply ensconced within opinion in the Society and about which a great deal has been thought, spoken and written. Here I would simply like to forget all these facts and approach the question again freshly. I can only hope that the reader wants to think along with the following thoughts.

In the year between the fire at the Goetheanum and the 'Christmas Conference', Rudolf Steiner spoke about the position of anthroposophy in the world, but also within the Society, the branches etc. From this it becomes clear that he was very unhappy about the situation. If one leaves aside all his reproaches that are connected with more external factors, *one* very severe reproach remains, namely that

> 'In this third period something started to develop that I want to call an inner opposition against that which I have to do myself in the Anthroposophical Society, a certain inner opposition. Naturally, most people are astonished when I speak about this inner opposition, because they are not aware of their own inner opposition, at least many are not. But I want to say: it is all the worse for that.'[42]

So it happened that there were circles of members that had begun to oppose Rudolf Steiner himself. It may be clear that this corresponds to an opposition to anthroposophy, and the same applies the other way round.

Then preparations were made for the 'Christmas Conference' and the refounding of the Society. In November 1923 Rudolf Steiner travelled to the Netherlands and said to Dr. Zeylmans von Emmichhoven (according to the re-

---

[42]   Rudolf Steiner, GA 258, p.135

port of Jan van Wettum): [43]

> *'What do I have to do? Must I found a kind of order with the friends who truly understand me? And work with great energy with this order into the world?' Then he raised his hands and the number of friends who truly understood him was smaller than the number of fingers that were raised. 'Or must I continue with all of them?' (there were at that time already several thousand members spread around the world.)'*

Clearly he did the latter. What was the significance of this deed?

The only human being, who represented anthroposophy as 'movement' was Rudolf Steiner himself. Because he adopted the chairmanship of the newly-founded Society, he led this movement – i.e. real anthroposophy – into the Society. In doing so, he of course introduced himself into the Society and connected himself to it. The spirit, however, cannot connect itself to a given Society just like that. The spirit always needs to be able to go through an intermediary. There must be something present that connects the spirit and the body, also when the body is a Society. The spirit needs the right *form*. One can think this over and understand it oneself but one can also find it confirmed by a statement from Rudolf Steiner:[44]

> *'It is true that it is a question of the spirit of a thing and not the form of it. But just as the form is void without the spirit, so would the spirit be incapable of deeds, if it did not create a form for itself.'*

Statutes can never create a form for the spirit; that can

---

[43] *Rudolf Steiner in Nederland*, 3, Jan van Wetum, Zeist

[44] Rudolf Steiner, GA 10, p.79

only be done through the right thoughts in a human being or a group of human beings. Thus it is thought that
builds a form for the spirit. Which thought? It can only
be the Foundation Stone. The Foundation Stone was the
form through which Rudolf Steiner connected himself to
the Society.

Yet this form alone is not enough, because it too could
be merely earthly, intellectual. Here, the issue was about
anthroposophers; they had to *know* what was about to happen within them through the foundation stone or else they
would have given up their freedom unconsciously. Thus
the form had to be understood in its meaning; a *being
aware of the form and its significance* was needed, in order
to be able to handle the events of the 'Christmas Conference'. Only in this way can the form turn into spiritual
power that can take up the spirit. This was especially what
the members of the Society had to cultivate within themselves. The Foundation Stone was the intermediary for the
movement. It could only be this, however, if the Executive
Council (Vorstand) was fully aware of it, and if afterwards
a large enough number of members were fully aware of it.
If not, the spirit had to withdraw. And this it had to do.

What does this mean?

It is not really so hard to understand *what* the members
actually failed to do. One can grasp it in one's contemplation; the answer lies very close to the question. What was
not strong enough was a full understanding of the individuality that lived in Rudolf Steiner. He was *not* understood
at all. During the 'Christmas Conference' he indicated in
his lectures who he was and what that meant. There were
several members who understood that he was talking about
himself and Ita Wegman.

However, the 'inner opposition' won the day. It was not

(permanently) understood with whom they were dealing, how great this individuality was, nor how extensive was his task. The Foundation Stone should have been connected with this consciousness. That was not the case, and *it still is not*, however much the Vorstand wants to have us believe that the 'Christmas Conference', the Foundation Stone and the Mantras of the First Class of the Free High school for Spiritual Science are still effective.

In the beginning, it seemed that the impulse of the 'Christmas Conference' had been taken up. On the 26th of April 1925 Ita Wegman wrote[45]:

'... *The Anthroposophical Society, which sent its members in great numbers to the 'Conference', certainly grasped the measure of the situation, were enthused and warmed and gave their agreement, and many, yes, most gave a sacred promise to assent to the new situation and serve the Master with new forces, with new feeling and willing.*
...
It was in Paris, when for the first time, he could share with the members present, who were only present in small numbers, the message that was so important, the message that the stream of the spiritual revelations had not stopped, and that the spiritual forces graced the Anthroposophical Society with spiritual bounties with even greater benevolence than before.'

And on the 19th of April 1925 (three weeks after Rudolf Steiner's death)[46]:

'*We must now prepare for the time in which an earthly task will be assigned to him again, and this time will come soon. We want to*

---

[45] Ita Wegman, *An die Freunde*, Natura Verlag Arlesheim

[46] Ibid.

be strong and hope and try to receive his spiritual intentions from the spiritual world. We feel him among us, the most wonderful and splendid human being, the Friend of God.'

At least there was one person who fully recognized his individuality.

But what did it mean to Rudolf Steiner himself that he connected to the Society?

Of course, this did not only have an effect from him towards the Society; the effect was also present the other way around. The form had not turned into spiritual force, and thus the anthroposophical spirit could not continue to stream downwards; it was stopped, pushed back. Eventually it had to retreat to its home, the spiritual world.

The Society of that time, an outward institution, had obviously nothing to do with the karma of Rudolf Steiner outwardly. Although the institution has been preserved since then, it is not a living being, thus it has no karma in that sense[3]. *People* have karma, and the striving of these people, as far as it is anthroposophical, has a karma. Every human being who elevates himself to the consciousness of pure form, in the sense of the Master of the Occident, irrefutably finds the individuality of this Master as a friend next to him. He feels the connecting karma. The form *must*, however, be a force, or else it does not guide the spirit. Everywhere where a consciousness of the form of anthroposophy – a sense of the pure form of thinking – is present, the Master of the Occident is there. The General Anthroposophical Society, however, in no way meets this requirement, because this requirement calls for a full understanding of the individuality of the Master, this Friend of God. One could perhaps still have had a *belief* in the connection between the Master and the Society in the eighties, but since 1998 this connection simply no longer exists. In the Netherlands an examination of 'racist' and 'discriminating' statements in the Collected Works (Gesamtausgabe) of Rudolf Steiner was conducted, which led to the Society's Executive Council (Vorstand) agreeing publicly in 1998 that there actually were such statements in his work. The Society consists of leaders who have not stood up for the integrity of the Master and of members who simply let this happen and still let it happen. Without a spiritual form, there is no connection between the Society and the Master.

This must now be a heavy burden on the spiritual works of the Master, because he can only work where there are human beings who understand what is expected of them.

It ought not to happen - as the Catholic Church does with Christ - simply to proclaim dogmatically that Rudolf Steiner has connected his karma with the Society. However, when one studies the history of the Society after the death of Rudolf Steiner, it even becomes impossible to follow and understand this dogma of the karmic connection. One really has to draw the conclusion that Rudolf Steiner turned away from the Society a long time ago. Not from the individual human being!

Ita Wegman, 1934:[47]

> 'Unfortunately, esotericism could not be understood by the people. It was all presumed to be self-evident and as if one had the right to it. What was meaningful and new about it - for that there was, apart from a few exceptions, little idea. Rudolf Steiner had much to be

---

[47]   Peter Selg, *Geistiger Widerstand und Überwindung*, (Spiritual Resistance and How to Overcome It), p.94

anxious about. This could not end well. And so he became ill. When an initiate falls ill, other laws apply than with ordinary human beings. By himself, an initiate can not fall ill; neither can he fall ill through his karma any more, he has left that behind.'

Peter Selg:

Over and over again Wegman indicated in her notes the necessity to deal intensively with the 'karma of the Christmas Conference', with its pre-history, its way of working, but also with its final earthly ruin by the prorogation of the Vorstand in its karmic configuration that was finally executed in Dornach. (First of all, we need to realize that the 'Christmas Conference' is actually kaputt, ruined.[48])'

And Marie Steiner wrote in 1944:[49]

'... And yet the 'Christmas Conference' is at the same time connected to an infinite tragedy. Because one cannot say anything else but that we were indeed called, but not chosen. We were not mature enough for the call. Further developments have shown that.
At first, everyone who participated in this 'Conference' felt lifted out of himself, inwardly warmed, and at the same time astonished. But a destiny hung over the whole event that will have to be borne out in other spheres of existence. The result showed what it meant for Dr. Steiner to take our karma upon himself.
In that lies the deep esoteric meaning that is connected to every sacrifice. Not the meaning that one usually gives to the words 'esoteric council'. The deepest esoteric meaning could consist in bringing to a harmonious balance earlier, previously divergent spiritual streams in some of their representatives. That would have been an esoteric task that could have been solved in collaboration with Rudolf

---

[48] These are words of Ita Wegman, quoted by Peter Selg

[49] Rudolf Steiner, Foreword in GA 260.

Steiner through his superior insight, force and capacity for love. But our human karma and the karma of the Society was loaded onto him – and immediately after the end of the 'Christmas Conference'. For on the last of those days, on 1ˢᵗ January 1924, he suddenly fell very ill. It was like a sword thrust, that struck his life at that social gathering, mentioned on the programme as a 'Rout', that was connected to a tea-party and the ingredients belonging to that. Still, he kept continuously and excessively busy until 28ᵗʰ September, the last day he spoke to us. His declining physical forces were nurtured and carried by a spiritual fire and outspent themselves. However, at the end, after his superhuman achievements in September, the power of the inner flame consumed him too. The 'Christmas Conference' stands in this tragic light for one who has the possibility to overlook what happened. We do not have the right to turn away from the gravity and the sorrow of this event. For from sorrow comes knowledge; it is born from pain. And this pain must lead us to seize hold of our task with an even stronger will.'

If the spiritual anthroposophical movement – carried by Rudolf Steiner as individuality – was to have remained connected to the Society, it would have been necessary that this Society be a harmonious group of people who would have made this connection possible. One must place that clearly before one's soul. If the Society is led by an esoteric Vorstand, that means that this group would have to make it possible that the spirit can stream into the Society the Vorstand would have to be a unity. It should not be governed by equality or monotony, but harmonic consonance, even if sometimes interrupted by dissonances – such cannot be avoided in human society. If this Vorstand, which was supposed to be a gateway for the spirit, carried on its relations with such bitter antipathy, as actually happened, then how could one seriously think that the esoteric current was still present or that Rudolf Steiner was still connected to the Society?

A society is something that consists of individuals, *and it is through this fact* that it is an organism, not through anything else. If it is a union because of something other than free individuals, it is a sect. In 1923, in the time of preparation before the foundation of the new Society, Rudolf Steiner said about this:[50]

'What sense does it make, if we tell people over and over again that we are not a sect, but then act as if we were one? For, you see, what must be understood above all by the members of the Anthroposophical Society is the primary condition for a Society in the modern era. A Society can in no way be a sect. Therefore, if the Anthroposophical Society is to stand on its right ground, no notion of 'we' may ever in fact play a role with regard to views within the Society. Over and over again one hears anthroposophers saying to the outside world: we, the Society, have this or that opinion. This or that happens to us. We want this or that. – That was possible in earlier times, that societies presented themselves before the world in such conformity. It is no longer possible in our time. In our time every individual human being must be a truly free human being in such a society. Every individual has views, thoughts and opinions. The [Anthroposophical] Society has no opinion. And that must already be expressed in the spoken idioms of someone who talks about the Society. The 'we' must actually disappear.'

Before that, however, he had said the following, which must be placed along with the foregoing in one's thoughts.[51]

'Therefore above all, one must seek to create the fundamentals for oneself in the different areas, but really to create these from the centre of anthroposophy, from the central sources.

---

[50]   Rudolf Steiner, GA 258, p.144

[51]   Ibid., p.140

*And if after the war the effort is made to take hold of all kinds of
practical life tasks, world tasks, then it would again be a matter of
bringing to life everything from the core of anthroposophy and of
understanding that right now it is least of all possible to compromise
on such practical life tasks. The one single thing is to say to the world
what is to be said from the anthroposophical centre, and then to
wait for how many people have an understanding for it.'*

These views did not change because of the 'Christmas
Conference', they were supposed to become really fundamental from that time onwards. On the one hand, the demand was made to work purely from the anthroposophical
centre, without compromises, that is, from a consciousness
of pure anthroposophical form. On the other hand, the
Society is made up of a number of free individuals. Within
this field of tension the esoteric current was supposed to
flow.

After the death of the Master both principles got lost.
Pure form could not be maintained, because it was poorly
acknowledged, understood and conceived. Freedom was
completely forgotten even among the members of the Vorstand.

Recently, a book appeared that was written by Erdmuth Jo-
hannes Grosse, *'Das Rätsel des Urvorstandes'*[52] (The Riddle of
the Original Vorstand). The book describes the conflicts in the
original Vorstand at length. At the end of the book the author
comes to a mild judgment of the errors and imperfections of
the members of the ,original Vorstand'. Of course it is nice
to experience it in this way – but it makes it more difficult

---

[52]   Erdmuth J. Grosse, *Das Rätsel des Urvorstandes* (The Riddle of the Original
Executive Council), Verlag am Goetheanum, 2007

to understand that there was a total ruin of the 'Christmas Conference'. Who bears the blame for that is not for us to judge. We can leave a judgment of that to the divine powers, irrespective of whether it was, or still is, mild or hard. What, however, we have to understand ourselves is that the spirit of anthroposophy is not there in the Society and cannot be there, because it cannot live, because the conditions are not there for it to do so. Whoever has created within himself the pure form of anthroposophy will be able to experience this himself. It cannot live in the Society; it is not tolerated there. The necessary living air that is needed for such a form is not present. It is excluded or else is furiously opposed; it is never received and is not allowed even to be called by its name. There is nothing in the Society that corresponds to this form.

The result of this is that the Foundation Stone and the Class Lessons cannot simply be used for meditation any more. As the content of knowledge they are still valuable and shall remain valuable. But as mantras they are not only inert, they are even harmful for the healthy life of the soul, if this soul has no spiritual experience. Therefore the Master himself warned often enough: the mantras becoming known outside the School [of Spiritual Science] would render them ineffective. Only with abstract thinking could one think that these mantras are only words. However, they are not only words. All the conflicts, all the competition, the whole striving for power that prevailed among the Class Readers and the members of the School at that time still lives on now; it has carried over into the mantras and flowed into them. They are weighed down with competitive spiritual beings, and one who has awakened the spirit inside himself experiences this and finally sees it too.

I know that I am saying something awful with this, but the truth can be awful. One who wants to experience this truth himself must thoroughly study the 'Denkschrift'[53] and then with that in mind consider that with the attitude that made this Denkschrift possible, Class Lessons were read out. With regard to this 'Denkschrift' J. Zeylmans writes[54]:

> *The book [the 'Denkschrift'] and the effect that it had on the 14th of April, namely, the provision of grounds for the exclusion of about two thousand members of the General Anthroposophical Society, have become a taboo subject since then in the historical writings of this Society.'*

One can also try to experience deeply the effect of meditating on the Class Lessons. One will become aware how one enters the processes of anti-anthroposophy, how it is impossible to find pure form among all the demonic effects, how these work as poison. Beings of competition and jealousy work through it.

Abstractly, one can of course be enthusiastic about the 'wonderful' Class Lessons. However, if one's thinking is really '*alive*', one can only focus with the deepest seriousness on what is experienced and draw conclusions from that.

In short, I would like to say: every human being who sees something justified in anthroposophy must concentrate on the individuality of the founder, on Rudolf Steiner. Then he must learn to experience that what he accomplishes in anthroposophy himself, whether it is knowing or acting or experiencing or love, has an effect on the Master. It does not make a difference whether one is a member of a Society or not, this

---

53 This ,Denkschrift' was published in 1935, before the expulsions of that year. The history of the events after Rudolf Steiners death are described in it from a very extreme point of view. Ita Wegman seems to be blamed for every failure

54 J.E. Zeylmans van Emmichhoven, Wer war Ita Wegman? (Who Was Ita Wegman?), Vol.3, p.259f.

is not important at all. It is the connection with anthroposophy that is the point. It connects the karma of this person with the karma of the Master of the Occident. And we should all inscribe deeply in our souls that our knowing, experiencing, acting and our love affect the karma of the Master. May each person seek the place where he can work with the greatest purity, where he can practise in love, so that the Master can return as a teacher and found for us a new esoteric Society! Thus an association will arise even now, because we are striving together, even if we never meet each other!

I shall close my thoughts with some words by Ita Wegman[55], not because I would have chosen her side in the battle, but because I find in her words exactly what I experienced in my fourteen years of membership of the Society.

'All ancient forms, even the latest form for anthroposophy, are basically broken, and it now seems to me as if one no longer has to search for a form for the life of anthroposophy anymore, but that every human being is that form himself, with which anthroposophy wants to unite. Where this happens, people will find each other and join together, in order to become a member of the true spiritual association. The (General Anthroposophical) Society is no longer needed, because anthroposophy already exists on earth. Now it is about individuals, and they have to build together from their development a higher association, which has its roots in the spiritual world. Every individual development is protected by this, every freedom of the individual person, and through his own insight, the individual person feels connected to this spiritual association or Michael School. This is how it has sounded within my soul. It is about my own stance within this impulse. All the rest will look after itself.'

---

55   Peter Selg, *Geistiger Widerstand und Überwindung*, (Spiritual Resistance and How to Overcome It), p.201

The Society and anthroposophy after 1925

That the spiritual observation that Rudolf Steiner took his esoteric stream back into the spiritual world because it had been insufficiently taken up by the members corresponds to the truth, is borne out in the events that occurred after Rudolf Steiner's death.

If the leading anthroposophers, the members of the Vorstand, had truly carried the esoteric stream inside themselves, the situation could never have come to this complete break-down. The outer circumstances, the characters, the opinions etc can be various. However, if this esoteric stream had flowed into every personality, it would have connected them deeply to each other. But it flowed away, and thus the Vorstand became a corpse, given over to the natural forces of decomposition. These are forces of separation which are terribly strong. And so what happened had to happen: the Vorstand was broken apart, and the various astral forces became free.

Ita Wegman was the closest to the esoteric stream; she had a deep notion that Rudolf Steiner was still concerned for his work on earth. He could also have participated from the spiritual world if people had finally become inwardly active. But the people strove for externals; they wanted to maintain the outer appearance of anthroposophy on earth. More and more, however, the inner life got lost. This went unnoticed, and even today people still do not want to acknowledge it to be true. What we have today as anthroposophy is a dead statue, a mummy. It perfectly resembles its living side in an external way, but it is ineffective, lifeless. The Society is a corpse, only an outer institution for the maintenance of the dead image – and apparently more and more for its total destruction. There is no anthroposophical movement; there is no Rudolf Steiner as initiator.

SECOND PART

How does one find a relation to the living Rudolf Steiner?

For most people of the materialistic era it is becoming hard to believe in a non-sensory existence – because we can not observe it with our senses. What the senses show us gives us certainty. For the rest, we do indeed have logic, which can prove to us – when we think harder – that supersensory and subsensory realms do exist, but we still do not hold the proofs of logic to be as valid as our sensory observation. 'The senses do not deceive, only the judgement deceives' says the wise Goethe. says. That is true. However, when understanding moves in purely logical contexts, it errs just as little as the senses, because it then also moves, in a 'sense', in the logical concept sense. There is no longer any doubt that pure thinking exists. However, every human being must master this first – and who takes pains to do so, or at least comprehends that he must take such pains?

But that is at the same time the greatest tragedy of death. The loved one leaves his body behind on earth, which quickly falls apart. He himself is not visible anymore, and to us who are left behind, he does not really exist anymore. It may be logically completely certain that the loved one must still be there, in our feelings we may still sense him – but that does not give us the certainty of his existence that sensory observation gave us. Peoples in cultures that are not so locked into a materialistic reasoning have a different relation to death. They also feel grief for the worldly loss, but at the same time they also celebrate release from the body, and for them, the deceased has not fully disappeared from life.

'Death as transformation of life' said Rudolf Steiner. He died a long time ago himself, and the question rises: is there a possibility of coming in contact with the real, existing Rudolf Steiner? Without losing oneself in fantasies, and without losing certainty? This question is of course valid for the connection to every deceased person – but it takes on a different meaning with regard to Rudolf Steiner.

If one is not clairvoyant and nevertheless wants to be in touch in a real way with this individuality who in his last incarnation bore the name Rudolf Steiner, one first needs to get to know this individuality profoundly, how he was, *spiritually*, in his last incarnation. One cannot do this with one's family, friends or acquaintances, because the *spiritual* part of these people is more hidden, more sunk in daily life. A man like Rudolf Steiner, however, gives a possibility to do this. In the first part I have tried to give a short summary of my acquaintance with Rudolf Steiner. It is based on published documents and lectures. In a certain way, one becomes acquainted with him extensively after studying these works. But has one truly found the *being* of this person? One has found the achievements of this being, which are built so magnificently on the fundaments of his being and what has revealed itself through them. But what about the being itself? Has one recognised it even in the simplest way? Names do not help here; the being has a name that can no longer be used in the earthly world. We can speculate about it, but only a spiritually seeing consciousness would be able to find the truth.

Pure thinking cannot help here either because it does not have the possibility yet to recognize something spiritual outside itself. But what one can do, is follow the indication that Rudolf Steiner gave at the beginning of his book *Rid-*

dles of the Soul [56].

This indication gives a lesson in truthfulness. Pure thinking strongly asks itself a question ... and experiences its own profound incapacity to be able to provide or receive an answer in any way at all. In this case pure thinking asks after the being of Rudolf Steiner – and finds nothing whatsoever. But what it does find is incapacity, and this leads the pure soul to the boundary of its existence, where it now has to endure its incapacity. This is contemplation, a helpless struggle at the abyss of one's own soul boundary.

And there finally, one does get a kind of answer. The answer can for now only be composed from the knowledge that one's own soul has already gained. The answer contains nothing 'new'; only the manner and form are new. The insights arrange themselves in an original way, unexpectedly, and one knows with a certainty equal to sensory certainty: here is the answer presented in the appearance of insights I have already gained.

In this case: here it is the original being of the individuality that was Rudolf Steiner, which gives the answer. But it can only speak through concepts that are already present.

The question about the being of Rudolf Steiner is the question about the red thread that goes through all the incarnations of this individuality, and that never breaks; that is over and over again the basis for his earthly work; that indeed transforms itself in a form suitable for the time, but that nevertheless is unchanging; that cannot be found with sensory eyes and combinatory reasoning, because then one

---

[56]   See n.34

gets hopelessly stuck in all the outer threads.

The human being has an essence – and this essence is different in every human being. This essence, which winds its way through incarnations like a red thread, which is also the guiding star between death and rebirth, pointing to the being constantly, is the core of the deepest striving of this being and at the same time also its eternal task. And when one has to do with such a masterly person as Rudolf Steiner this essence is truly *pronounced*. If the researcher already knows what has been thus pronounced, without having seen it so clearly and meaningfully in this connection before, it links itself - in the real incapacity that one is feeling - to an answer.

The philosopher said:[57]

> *'Consequently, the divine spirit thinks itself, if it is the most perfect, and its thinking activity consists of thinking about thinking. Now apparently, knowledge, sensory observation, belief, reasoning as a rule direct themselves towards something else and only on exception towards themselves. But when thinking and being thought are two things, one asks oneself, where does the God's perfection lie, in its thinking or in its object? Because both are not the same. But isn't it so that in several fields knowledge is its own object? In the forms of creative knowledge it is, apart from matter, substance and concept, and in theoretical forms of knowledge it is reason and thinking. Since what has been thought and thinking power are not different, as far as the immaterial is concerned, so therefore will also thinking and what has been thought coincide in the divine spirit.'*

And:

---

[57]   Aristotle, *Hauptwerke*, translated (into German) by Wihlem Nestle, 1997

134

*'But thinking in itself has the best in itself as its object, and abso-
lute thinking has the absolute best as its object. Thus, the thinking
force (spirit) thinks itself, because it participates in the object of
thinking. Due to the fact that it namely understands and thinks its
object, it becomes the object of thinking itself, so that thinking force
and thought fall together. The thinking force is namely the ability
to take in what has been thought and the actual being. And it is
present when it does that. This actuality is thereby on a yet higher
level the divine, which the thinking force seems to be one with,
than the capacity for perception, and the best and most enjoyable is
actual thinking. If God is always in this condition, which is only
temporarily possible for us, then that is already beautiful; but if he
is it on a higher level, it is even more beautiful. And so it is indeed.
And also life comes from him. Because the energy of the spirit is life,
the spirit is energy. God's absolute energy is the best and eternal life.
We thus state that God is an eternal, complete being, and from Him
come life and unbroken eternal existence. That is God...'*

And the saintly philosopher:[58]

*'The second difference between our word (concept) and the divine
word consists in that our word is imperfect; but the divine word is
the most perfect. Because we cannot express all our thoughts in one
word we must use many imperfect words, with which we can partially express what lies in our knowing. But with God it is not so:
because he thinks himself and all the rest that he thinks through his
being in one moment, the only divine word is an expression of all
that, which is inside God – not only the divine persons, but also the
creatures: otherwise it would be imperfect. That is why Augustine
says: 'If there would be less in God's words than in the knowing of
the one who speaks, the word would be imperfect; but it is certain,
that it is the most perfect: so it is the one single thing there is. In Job*

---

58   St. Thomas Aquinas, Super Evangelium St. Johanni Lectura.

33:14 is written: God speaks once.'

And:

'Secondly we can conclude from what has been presented that the word (concept) always proceeds from the spirit in a living process of thinking, and further, that the word is always the concept and an image of the object that is thought about. If thinking and thought are the same, then the word is the concept and an image of the spirit from which it originates; but if the thinking and the thought are different, then the word is not an image and not the concept of the thinking (spirit), but of the thought object, as the imagination that someone has of a stone is only an image of the stone. But if the spirit thinks itself, then in this we have to do with an image and the concept of the spirit. Therefore Augustine supposes that there be an image of the Trinity (of God) in the (human) soul, insofar as the spirit thinks itself, not however, insofar as it thinks something else. Accordingly, it is clear, that one must presume the word in every spiritual being; because from the concept of thinking it follows that the spirit forms something through thinking; this forming is called the word. On this basis one must accept the word in all thinking.'*

The spiritual scientist:[59]

Thus far we have arrived at the following truths. At the first stage of our contemplation of the world, the whole of reality confronts us as an unconnected aggregate; thinking is included within this chaos. If we move about within this manifoldness, we find one part in it which, already in the form of its first appearance, has the character the other parts have yet to acquire. This part is thinking. What is to be overcome in the rest of experience, namely the form of its immediate appearance, is precisely what we must hold onto with

---

[59]   See n.6, p. 46f.

136

thinking. Within our consciousness we find this factor of reality, our thinking, that is to be left in its original form, and we are bound up with it to such an extent that the activity of our spirit is at the same time the manifesting of this factor. It is one and the same thing, looked at from two sides. This thing is the thought-content of the world. On the one hand it manifests as an activity of our consciousness, on the other as a direct manifestation of a lawfulness complete in itself as a self-determined ideal content. We will see right away which aspect has the greater importance.

Now, because we stand inside this thought-content, because we permeate it in all its component parts, we are in a position really to know its very nature. The way it approaches us is a guarantee of the fact that the characteristics we earlier ascribed to it really are due to it. Therefore, it can certainly serve as a starting point for every further kind of contemplation of the world. From this thought-content itself we can conclude what its essential character is; but if we wish to determine the essential character of anything else, we must begin our investigations with this thought-content. Let us articulate this still more clearly. Since we experience a real lawfulness, an ideal certainty, only in thinking, the lawfulness of the rest of the world, which we do not experience from this world itself must also lie already contained in thinking. In other words: manifestation to the senses and thinking stand over against each other in experience. The first, however, gives us no enlightenment about its own essential being; the latter gives us enlightenment both about itself and about the essential being of the manifestation to the senses.

And:[60]

'We have said that Aristotle has pointed out that we must distinguish between what is form and what is matter with everything

---

[60] Rudolf Steiner, *Philosophy and Anthroposophy*, GA 35. Lecture of 1908

we meet in the circle of our experience. Now one may say: in the knowledge process we approach form in the manner just described. But is there also a possibility to approach what is material? N.b.: Aristotle understands by the material not only the touchable, but substance, the spiritual element which also underlies reality. Is there a possibility of understanding not only what floats from things to us but also of entering into things, to identify oneself with matter? This question is also important for epistemology. It can only be answered by those who have gone deeply into the nature of thinking, pure thinking. One must first rise to this concept of pure thinking. Aristotle states that we can see pure thinking as an actuality. It is pure form; it is, as it first appears, without content regarding the immediate, individual things in the sense world outside.

…

Where, within pure thinking, is there a way not only to create form, but matter at the same time as form? As soon as we have something which creates matter together with form, then we can connect to a solid point, epistemologically speaking. We are everywhere, for example, when we construct a circle, in a special case, so that we must say: what I say about this circle, is objectively correct; whether it is applicable to things depends on their showing, when I come across them, if they bear the laws within them that I have constructed. When the sum of all the forms dissolves in pure thinking, something must be left over, which Aristotle calls matter, if it is not possible to arrive at such a reality from pure thinking itself.

Aristotle can be completed by Fichte here. In the sense of Aristotle one can first come to the formula: ‚everything around us, as well as that which belongs to the invisible worlds, makes it necessary that we set what is material opposite the formal nature of reality. To Aristotle the principle of God is a pure actuality, a pure act, that means an act such that the actuality, thus the giver of form, has the power to bring forward its own reality, not to be something that confronts the material, but something that is at the same time in its own pure activity itself the full reality.

138

The image of this pure actuality is inside the human being himself, when, out of pure thinking, he comes to the concept of the 'I'. There he is in the I with something that Fichte calls 'Tathandlung' (lit. 'deed-handling', usually translated as 'self-positing'). He comes to something within him that, when it lives in actuality, brings its matter to expression at the same time along with this actuality. If we grasp the I in pure thoughts, we are in a centre where pure thinking at the same time essentially brings its material being to expression.

…

Thus, epistemologically, the sentence can be formulated: 'that also in pure thinking a point is attainable, where reality and subjectivity fully touch each other, where man experiences reality.' If he starts there and fertilizes his thinking so that it arises out of itself again from there, he grasps things from the inside out. Thus it is in the I that has been both conceived and at the same time created by a pure act of thinking that something is present through which we pierce through the boundaries that for all other things have to be placed between form and matter..'

Now one can of course easily raise the following objection: the fact that a human being becomes enthusiastic for something that was also enthusiastically discussed by previous thinkers does not prove that one has here to do with the same individuality, and not at all that this 'something' is a sign of an individual's essence. Rudolf Steiner could very well merely have adapted his knowledge from earlier philosophers. This, however, is an entirely materialistic objection. In such a world view everything stands next to everything else like stones: the philosopher has written something that died with him, but it was preserved in documents. Later thinkers occupied themselves with it, but the first did not work through into the last through a living effect.

This book does not adopt a materialist point of view. Insights are considered as living effects that continue to be effective beyond death. The later reader of the writings can be inspired by this living effect. But he can also himself be the 'originator' of the insights, i.e. the first one who attained them on earth. When the human being who had the *original* insight finds it again, it is something else. He does not repeat it, but causes it to grow further, appropriate to the new time.

To notice this development one must have an organ; intellect is not enough, because that is also only able to line up all the facts next to each other. An *experience* of thinking must be practised in order to be able to feel this *life* of insights. But then the later thought of the saintly philosopher – 'if thinking and thought are one and the same...'- is not simply taken over from the metaphysics of the ancient philosopher. The thought of the philosopher lives on; it has developed, so that it is not only applicable for the general concept of God, but also for the concept 'word': the concept can be thoroughly christianised. One has to learn to feel this very deeply. Not only up above 'in the frontal lobe', but with the whole, lively human being, without any kind of fantasising.

The philosopher was the first to make thinking itself into an object of knowledge. From this grew logic, which today has just the same validity as at that time. Thus just as Pythagoras discovered the law of the right-angled triangle, which still applies today, so the philosopher discovered the law of logic, the doctrine of the theorem (pure logic, 'peri Hermeneia'), the doctrine of the concept (the Categories). He did for the human context what he presents in his Metaphysics as the characteristic of God: the thinking of thinking.

We find this form of thinking again in the Scholastic. The saintly philosopher, the 'doctor angelicus', struggles with this concept of thinking. He is bound to the dogmas of the church; he must hold himself to Augustine and cannot release himself from this. Although he takes over the developed concepts of divine thinking and being from the philosopher, he cannot realize them. He is only allowed to apply his sharp, intelligent, versatile thinking in defence of Catholic principles. Although he *knows* that thinking can think about itself and that in doing so, it raises faith to science, he dare not develop this idea. Nevertheless, his whole theological philosophy (philosophical theology) is steeped with the superhuman force and power of intelligence. But at the same time at the end of his life he calls this work of intelligence 'mere straw'; in the light of Christ it means nothing to him. When one experiences all this, one feels how the whole life of this 'doctor angelicus' stood in the light of this insight - how he struggled with it but was unable to accomplish it. The materialist will say: Nonsense! The man simply learned that 'insight' from the ancient philosopher but he dared not become enthusiastic about it. On the contrary, a spiritual thinking and feeling find the essence of the philosopher in the doctor angelicus, not only as insight, but as further developed essence.

This essence appears again at the end of the 19th century. It speaks further developed words and works strongly for a spirituality – a knowing of God - that is built up on a rock solid fundamental principle that the true I is born when it rouses itself in freedom, not only to acknowledge the category of knowing but to *realize* it. This means that this category of knowing is a thinking that is actively conceived and resurrected. It is no longer logic, and there is no uncertainty about whether the human being may strive so high. It is the absolute certainty that knowing can become spiritual only when it applies its own category to itself, independent, without any other influence than one's own I, which comes into being only through this act. Ordinary cognition occurs through the soul. The cognition of knowing is a deed of the spirit.

One who wants to get to know Rudolf Steiner in his essence, must pause here. Here lies the fruit of the previous life. Here the development is led on further.

What is actually said with this? An essence is illumined, but what does this provide us with in order to find a relation to Rudolf Steiner? We must look still deeper. It may be clear that this individuality has an 'entelechy' *that lies very close to intelligence itself.*

There is a cosmic, superhuman power, a being that includes within itself an army of other beings at the same time, and that was in the past the regent of the cosmic intelligence. We must imagine this being as intensively and extensively as possible. The creating world-word, the divine trinity itself, creates *intelligently*. This creating includes everything that we can make our own through knowing – and much, much more. What we know inside us as intelligence is a part of this creating world-word.

This intelligence itself is a multitude of beings. We only know the ability to connect concepts in the right way with the observed reality and with each other. In this process we do not experience beings. Ancient wisdom, however, does describe this; Zarathustra, for example, speaks about twelve Amshaspands who one can truly interpret as 'concept- beings'. While we know twelve concept categories and a thirteenth, which is the category of knowing itself, we find in these Amshaspands the concept-categories as living beings. One must think of this in so *real* a way that one can grasp the thought that these living concepts, these concept-beings 'built' the human brain out of the cosmos. That is how real the world is! The human brain is an image of externalised category-beings. Therefore, it has this wonderful affinity with concepts, which in the mirror of the brain become thinking, because the brain is formed from thinking itself. As the eye is formed by the being of light, the brain is formed by living concepts.

Something else besides these beings, however, is the *activity* of intelligence, which is comparable to the difference between the content and form of thinking on the one hand, and the activity and capacity of thinking on the other hand. Only this constitutes human intelligence. So there is also a cosmic intelligence, which represents the *activity* of the connecting and disconnecting, the activity of finding connections.

So now it is not therefore about the 'what' but about the 'how'. The origin of this 'what' *and* 'how' is the creating world-word. The operative connection between everything that is 'what' is then the 'how', the intelligence.

If we compare this to a symphony orchestra, then the 'what' is the capable musicians with their different instruments. The intelligence is comparable to the performance of the symphony; the musicians' abilities are applied in order to make something actually tangible. The composer can be compared to the creating world- word, and the performance, brought about by capable musicians, is comparable to the active intelligence. But there must also be a regent of the intelligence. Here in this example it is the conductor. In the cosmos it was that heavenly power, composed from a whole army of heavenly beings, who had to manage the cosmic intelligence, the actual performance of the divine word.

143

Creative concept-beings shape the building stones of understanding in accordance with the model of the world-word and they work down into the physical, in that they build the brain. The conductor of this musical activity is the cosmic power who has to manage and direct the intelligence. In esoteric Christianity this power is called 'The archangel Michael'. Actually, we must never speak this name casually, but rather, think through and experience deeply, very deeply, whom we are actually referring to by it.

Now the human being, the child of God, is supposed to become independent and raise himself up towards freedom. A being can only be independent if it can judge on its own, if it is intelligent. And it can only become free if it learns to guide these judgments fully independently. Thus it is not to be influenced by influences from the outside, nor by influences from the spiritual world.

If man is to be at the same time independent and also free, two things would have to happen: intelligence must be given to man to use according to his own capacity; and the spiritual world must disappear from this independent consciousness, it must become invisible.

We know from daily life how it can go: the children grow up, move away and live by themselves, they are independent and no longer pay attention to the warnings of their parents. What will happen to them?

But let us first return to that essence: the understanding of the intelligence, whose ability to maintain itself becomes ever more conscious, because through cognition of intelligent activity, self-consciousness arises that is able to control intelligence. At this point the relationship of this essence, this entelechy, with the power that is called Michael, should be clear. In the cosmic sense, it was Michael who directed the intelligent activity. In Rudolf Steiner an entelechy was embodied, an individuality that had the characteristic of wanting to use the human, independent, intelligence self-consciously and the ability to do that. This noticeable ‚quality' therefore permeated the individuality of Rudolf Steiner: as Michael was the conductor of the cosmic intelligence, Rudolf Steiner is the masterly conductor of his own intelligence, and summons his contemporaries to develop this mastery in themselves also, because the time for it has come.

Rudolf Steiner is therefore a servant of Michael, a coworker of Michael.

This man has an intimate relationship with intelligence. As philosopher in ancient Greece, he cognizes the 'technique' with which it works. As saintly philosopher in the Middle Ages, in religious questions he practises the technique he had formerly cognized and falls into helplessness, because he reaches the possibility to acknowledge that intelligence could lead to the divine itself.

In this man intelligence lives in such a way that it can fully unfold itself. The being of this person is itself intelligent, it must be deeply connected to intelligence. In esoteric Christianity we found the regent of intelligence. Can we also find intelligence itself, in the form of a being? It would have to be found in a being that has a direct similarity with music. Because it is not the musicians, and also not the conductor, with whom we can compare intelligence itself – it is the sounding music itself, the sounding world-word. Where do we find this music shown in an image that at the same time shows us intelligence?

When one has developed a spiritual thinking, a thinking

that can think spirituality, then one takes all religious, spiritual and mystical images seriously. One knows: all these images are formed in accordance with true reality; they are all images of real beings.

Thus, in the Greek mythology we know of Apollo. He is the only god, as it were, in whom harmony rules: the God who is not ruled by human instincts and desires, but who is musical, harmonic and intelligent. In the saga of Prometheus we find a touching episode. Prometheus is punished by Zeus, because he has stolen fire from heaven and given it to man, in order to gain freedom. Zeus was prepared to forgive him if Prometheus would use his prophetic foresight in order to tell Zeus who would overthrow him. Prometheus refuses, and, chained to the Caucasus, has to suffer an eagle eating his liver for thousands of years. No being has the courage to ask Zeus to release him from his suffering; only Apollo tries, with the harmonic music of his harp. Zeus relents somewhat, because the quiet courage of Apollo, bathed in harmony, is a wonderful gift.[61]

The Plea of Apollo

See, how he who represented the powerful thinking of man, the ability to think ahead, has his body chained to the rock, unable to release himself from the chains, no longer in a position of being able to free himself at all. Limited to the miserable movements that are left for him while chained to the rigid stone, he has to let desire pick at him undisturbed and eat his divine body ... so as to allow healing to occur at night, and then the torture can start all over again by sunrise.

The moaning and complaining of Prometheus echoed between the

---

[61]   Mieke Mosmuller, *Prometheus*, Occident 2010

steep rocks rose up to the Gods on Olympus and to the Titans in the depths, where Prometheus' father Iapetos, filled with compassion, had to hear his son suffer. Other gods felt disgust at the fate of Prometheus, while there were also gods who mocked him and took malicious delight. But none of them dared to interfere in the decision of Zeus, the god of gods. His will was the strongest and with that his absolute power. Thus decades, hundreds, thousands of years of dreadful torments went by.

But there was one god, who could allow himself to come before Zeus, his father, and beg him from sincere pity, to end the suffering of Prometheus. Apollo, son of Zeus and Leto, born on the beautiful island Delos, was harmony itself, that underlies the muse of the divine spoken word. In the oracle of Delphi that he himself had founded, he transmitted the word of Zeus to man. Everything of him was – and is – harmony, consonance, rising above every desire. His instrument, the harp, is the visual and sound image of the harmony of its divine player. This profound harmony that is Apollo, does not hold back from entering where disharmony rules. One had better not oppose Apollo, because his harmony is divine, and not timid like that of humans...

Thus Apollo stepped in front of his father Zeus, accompanied by the horrible echoing complaints of Prometheus. Two holy women were standing by his side, on the one side his mother Leto ..., on the other side his sister Artemis. Both goddesses cried golden tears of compassion while Phoebus Apollo spoke:

'My lord, father Zeus, how long must the pitiful Prometheus moan under your divine punishment? Don't you feel mercy for this deep, apparently unending torture? Don't you hear the whole of humanity begging you to release him and send a liberator to him, the whole earth sounds with this begging question, in the rustle of the wind, in the streaming of the rivers, in the sound of the rising sun ... even in your thunder and lightning, in your storms the plea

147

seems to sound that I direct to you now, mighty ruler!'
Zeus considered the words of his beloved, highly-esteemed son in his
divine fatherly heart and spoke:
'Very well, I do not want to offer resistance to your words, which
sound as harmoniously as music. But I can not change my divine
decision either. Justice must be done to both, your words and my
decision.'
He was silent and the thundering sound of his voice rolled on for
some time more ... his eyes lightened with thoughts and he went on
with his divine speech:
'Then it is my will, that Prometheus be released. Let Heracles ac-
complish that task, but in such a way that the punishment that
was lain on him by me is not completely lifted. Someone must be
found who will take the place of Prometheus; Prometheus shall,
however be released, but still be chained to the rock of the Caucasus
forever...'

Apollo is the representative of reason, of justice. He speaks
through the Pythia in the oracle of Delphi, his statements
are intelligent and reliable. In that sense, they are not comparable to the fortune-telling of the Sybils, who tell the
truth one time and not the other. Apollo speaks in the sun-
oracle, from his harmonic sun-reason. In 'Vorstufen zum
Mysterium von Golgatha' (Approaching the Mystery of
Golgotha, GA 152) Rudolf Steiner describes how Apollo
plays an important role in keeping human intelligence on
the right track:[62]

'The Greeks, who in their mythology felt something like after-imag-
es of the events of the Atlantean epoch, expressed in that mythology
these supersensible facts I have just mentioned. And the image, the
after-image, under which the Greeks imagined a third ensoulment

---

[62]   Rudolf Steiner, *Vorstufen zum Mysterien Golgatha*, (Preliminary Stages of the
Mystery of Golgotha) GA 152, p.137

by Christ in an Angel-like being, is Apollo, the God of the Sun. Apollo as the protector of the statements of Pythia, appears as that being who harmonises the dragon that rises from the earth in the form of smoke. If this smoke were to flow in the passion of Pythia without the harmonising effect of Apollo, thinking, feeling and willing would be expressed as madness. Because of the impregnation with the forces of Apollo what Pythia has to say became at times the wisest advice that was given to the Greeks. If one could have asked an initiate in the ancient mysteries for his true opinion of who Apollo was, he would certainly have given the answer: he is the herald of Jesus Christ, who has not yet descended to the physical plane.'

'Humanity has received a wonderful imagination of this third Christ-event in the image of Saint George conquering the dragon, or the archangel Michael conquering the dragon. It is wonderful to be able to notice how this imagination of Saint George and the dragon is indeed an afterimage of the third transcendental Christ-event.'

Apollo is the intelligent one among the Greek gods, harmonious musical. In Orpheus his being comes to expression. The Orphic mysteries are mysteries of the word, as also are the mysteries of Ephesus.

From the correspondence between Rudolf Steiner and Ita Wegman we know which incarnations he found for both of them. The materialist will say: 'For who he considered himself to be.' However, the spiritual thinker can truly find the individuality again. Thus before the incarnation of Rudolf Steiner there was an earlier one among the ancient Greek philosophers. In that life he was the teacher of Plato, student of Socrates and initiated in the mysteries of the word at Ephesus. This initiation appears very clearly in the platonic dialogue, which bears the name of this man. Here, standing before Socrates he represents absolute faith in the rightness of a chosen word.

Cratylus:[63]

> 'For I am of the opinion, Socrates, that the correct explanation for
> this would be that there was a force greater than the human, which
> gave to things their first names and therefore they are necessarily
> correct.'

This trust in correctness is not only based on the sense, the
meaning of the word, it also has at its basis the building up
of the word from several vowels and consonants. The letters
have such an effect that the meaning already lies in this effect.
That is impressively outlined in this dialogue, obviously by
means of the Greek words, and also subjected to doubt, as
Socrates always does. Thus we find here an art of the word,
that is directly connected to the art of the concept.

The young man in conversation with Socrates here bears the
individuality that is related so intimately to intelligence. Here
he still shows how intelligence is directly connected to the
sounds that form the spoken word.

He was initiated in the mysteries of Ephesus. No abstract
word-knowledge was taught there, such as we, for example,
know as philology; the student was initiated into the for-
mative forces of the world-word. He learned how the spiritual soul forces of the word (forms) can work into earthly
substance (matter), shaping it. The vowels formed the inner,
soul aspect of this forming activity, the consonants the outer, earthly aspect. One could learn to experience the vowels
as seven strings on which the spirit plays, while the music

---

[63]   Plato, *Kratylos*, Rowohlts Klassiker

sounds in the box of the earth, which is an image of the fixed stars. And the seven essences of the wandering stars (planets), which are familiar in Greek mythology as seven gods, were transformed into the known metals in the earthly sphere.

This was all still true mystery-knowledge that was already no longer expressed in the incarnation of the ancient Greek philosopher. What remained was the logic as science of the word (of the concept) and a natural science that was han-ded down only in fragments and not completely.

*

There exists a Grail history 'Titurel' by Wolfram von Eschenbach. In it we find a reference to these insights in the creating, sounding world-word, as it could be recognized through the script of the fixed and the wandering stars.

The warning of Apollo, that intelligence has to follow the path of truth, that it must guard this road, get used to it and not relapse into old clairvoyance, but seek out the free, truth-loving intelligence, is represented in the dog 'Gardevias' (shepherd of the road). It wears a collar, in which the star writing can be read.

A young knight wants to get the dog for his lover, who wants to read the star writing on the collar, but he is killed during his journey. This event leads to the famous Grail image of the young woman with her dead lover on her lap. This is a Grail image for the Pieta, and it expresses the human tragedy that man has to renounce the star writing if he is to obtain freedom. The human soul can only carry the spirit in a dead form inside himself (as intellect).

In this image the entelechy that expresses itself over and over again in a form corresponding to a particular epoch, becomes clearly visible in a form suitable for the time of the Grail. In the incarnation as saintly philosopher the dead, intellectual intelligence must hold to the track of truth, but it can not yet resurrect.

Thus we have seen a similarity between individuality described here and the cosmic intelligence, which became human intelligence. This human intelligence could only be experienced as dead because of the freedom that was still to be attained. No symphony was heard, there was only a pattern, a schema left over. In this schema the saintly philosopher cannot acknowledge the divine.

But the spiritual scientist can. The cosmic power that bears the name 'Michael', has allowed the intelligence that it administered to come down to human beings. They obtain thereby an intelligence that becomes ever more independent. However, because this intelligence cannot be experienced as something living – for the sake of freedom - the question arises: will man with his intelligence guard the path?

The spiritual scientist incarnates in the age of the consciousness soul. That means that the soul becomes aware of itself and is then able to investigate ever more deeply its own sheaths and those of the spirit. Therein lies all the knowledge from earlier initiations, not recognizable by normal daily consciousness. The rebirth of the spirit, however, which becomes a fact through the realisation of the 'category of knowing', is at the same time the step that makes the investigation of subconscious knowledge possible – this works as something deathly if it remains unknown. The relation with Michael comes forward in this 'managing of one's own human intelligence' in the renewed, elaborated 'O Man, know yourself.'

The greatness and depth of intelligence, the care with which it is cognised, the exactitude with which 'the path is guarded', points to the divine gift of Apollo.

The individuality, the bearer of this essence, thus renews the fruit of the incarnation of the saintly philosopher. One should put this before one's soul over and over again clearly and intensely: the saintly philosopher, who in union with Christ had to declare all his intelligent research to be mere straw, this intelligent, humble, holy soul becomes now fully aware, fertilized by his own spirit. In this fertilization, which is the awakening of the whole development, he sees how it has become possible. All the knowledge that had died and was piled up in the soul resurrects through the act of spiritual self-knowledge, and the primal process of death and resurrection becomes visible: the spiritual scientist stands in 'the most earnest and solemn festival of knowledge' before the Mystery of Golgotha.

The creative world-word that gave itself to man was crucified, died and resurrected. The intelligence that has become schematic can also resurrect, if it has learned out of its own initiative to guard the path.

First know the solemn guardian
That stands at the gateway of the spiritual world,
Denying entrance to your senses' forces,
And to your intellect's power
Because you, weaving in senses and images of thought,
Free of the being of space
Free of time's power of illusion
Must first powerfully master
The truth of your own being.[64]

---

[64] Rudolf Steiner, *From the Contents of the Esoteric Class*, GA 266/3, p.503

153

This verse still sounds at the end of the life of this spiritual scientist, and it shows that he has not changed his relevant insights.

Only when, blind before the spiritual world, man has powerfully mastered the truth of his own being, can he become a spiritual scientist. This moment was fully realized for Rudolf Steiner around the turn of the 19th century.

His entire existing knowledge, also the nature and the way of knowing, is – for the moments of spiritual research – transformed. The spiritual scientist now gets into that state in which he can take in the actually present creative world-word into his intelligence and can find it again in resurrected form. The actual being of this man was already christianised before his last incarnation. Now his earthly intelligence, his free capacity for knowledge is christianised.

That he spoke and wrote against Christianity in his earlier years says nothing in this respect. Conventional, outer Christianity does not even come anywhere close to this christianising. The word is the same, but not the meaning in any way.

Thus a man stands there who was always connected to intelligence, who also carried within him the *mastery* of intelligence as a characteristic mark of his being. But now the living world-word itself enters into his intelligence. Once one has understood this, one is no longer surprised about the enormous labour of knowledge of this spiritual scientist. But one always stands 'in wonder' at it.[65]

---

[65]   J.W.Goethe, *Natural Scientific Writings. Lectures on Comparative Anatomy*, Poem

In the epistemology brought by Rudolf Steiner, we find once again Apollo, Michael and the Pietà, as they were once living in the philosopher and in the Grail stories. In eurythmy, speech formation, the dramatic arts, we find again the initiation in the mysteries of Ephesus. In the Christology lectures the philosopher-saint stands before us. In Rudolf Steiner's occult science we find mystery-knowledge in the robe of Christian resurrection.

The being of the living Rudolf Steiner is the resurrected, self-controlling intelligence. The name 'Rudolf Steiner', however, no longer allows one to experience this being. Through all kinds of connotations, a name receives a particular colour. For one who knows the name, a certain feeling comes with it. That quality depends on the relation to anthroposophy, to the Anthroposophical Society, but also on the reports in the news, that put a certain stamp on the perception.

So it is with everything and everyone; it cannot be avoided. But one may expect of people who call themselves students of this spiritual scientist and who are supposed to love him ardently that they will not rest before they have cleared his name from all stain. They can only do that if they form images and concepts of the actual true being of the Master through meditative power and pure thinking. He has been the Master of the Occident already through many incarnations. If such an image, such a concept, as I have now formed, were to be cherished radiantly in the hearts and minds of anthroposophers, the Goetheanum would be a sun-temple, a mystery centre of the earth –

and the Master of the Occident would be able to take up his leadership there again, now or in a couple of decades, when he would be on earth again.

THIRD PART

After the death of the spiritual scientist

In order to find a relation to the being of Rudolf Steiner, it is important to imagine as clearly as possible how the parts of his being developed further after death.

His physical body is, like that of every other human being at death, given over to the earth, to earthly forces. This involves not only the decay of his body, but also of his name. Up to his death it was Rudolf Steiner. But when he returns to his spiritual home, the name has become the name of one of his many incarnations. That is the first thing that we should take good note of. 'Rudolf Steiner' is often seen as a kind of possession of the Society, the possession of anthroposophers.

The fact that he taught us himself that an initiate, as it were, keeps his personality, seems to justify this. But one has to distinguish that he renewed his whole knowledge in the incarnation of Rudolf Steiner; he resurrected in the spirit. The condition for this was, amongst others, that the personality was so purified that it could not give way to the individuality. And because his whole resurrected knowledge revealed itself in this purified personality, one can expect that it becomes eternal. But it does not become eternal as Rudolf Steiner; that would be a restriction of the development. The personality in the spiritual sense is nevertheless something other than the appearance of the earthly personality with its biography, its appearance etc.

Just as the resurrected physicality relates to the earthly body, so the resurrected personality relates to the worldly personality. The resurrected personality strongly resembles the being, the essence, the entelechy. This being has a name, a 'mystery name', which was discussed in the previous chapter. This name is not Rudolf Steiner; that decays with the end of the earthly life of Rudolf Steiner. This release from the name is a real release.

All nuances, connotations, judgments etc. that arise in connection with the name Rudolf Steiner do not apply anymore to this being, who lives on in his spiritual home and is welcomed there with true judgment.

In 2007 a DVD was released with the title: 'Rudolf Steiner, The Versatile Outsider – a Portrait.' This film portrays the life and work of Rudolf Steiner. Anyone who has an interest in Rudolf Steiner should see this movie once in order to get an idea of how one can use this medium to present an image of *death*, of a dead personality. The whole recording breathes death, the images, the reciter's voice, the way in which Rudolf Steiner is presented. It is a dead archive. However, there are several living people talking about Steiner, and *one* man even shows real enthusiasm. Nevertheless, these people have also fallen into the shadow of death that hangs over the film. The image of death goes on through it until the real death of Rudolf Steiner, thus until 1925. One even sees the corpse of Rudolf Steiner, how he lies there, completely hollow, with his striking head.

With this, essentially, at least *one* true image has been shown: that there is no further development after 1925. Things can only be repeated in the mood of voices at the graveside. Not only has anthroposophy been preserved as a mummy, Rudolf Steiner's spirit has also been mummified, insofar as far as one has managed to catch something of it. He has remained like he was last seen; Rudolf Steiner is a preserved corpse.

When one sincerely and intensely experiences the effect of such a DVD, the only thing that can happen is that such a corpse explodes. The enormous being of the deceased spiritual scientist will not allow himself to be locked up in such a prison. He releases himself from it, expands and lets the meditating human beings experience *who* he actually is.

In the earthly incarnation one can experience different forms of the actual individual being in his physical-etheric body. Such a DVD, as characterized above, puts only *one* incarnation under the magnifying glass and makes it stiffen into a permanent shape. The true human being, however, releases himself from his embodiment over and over again and is born into a world that is the 'medium' for spiritual incarnations. What I mean to say is that lives between death and a new birth enable themselves to be experienced also as a whole; they are not only a sort of sleep, but together they are a real existence. Man enters this existence after death. There he unites himself with his own actual being, adds the good fruits of his past earth life to it and reshapes the bad fruits.

A man like Rudolf Steiner enriches his being and thereby enriches every spiritual being with that. After his death he finds not an undifferentiated 'something'; he finds his being as it has become through all his earthly incarnations and through the spiritual 'between-life' states. His being does not have the name Rudolf Steiner. This name is only a part of the being. His spiritual being also lives a 'life', has been through all kinds of experiences in the spiritual world and has also achieved much. In this world time has another form. On earth time passes as it were in a line; it is, in a matter of speaking, an extended part of a circle, so that it looks like a straight line. If one takes a closer look, the line even becomes a sort of collection of points, in which future and past 'roll together' to present time.

Past

Future

Present

In the spiritual world, beyond the etheric world, this time expires. It becomes a completeness, in which past, present and future are present in *one*. Like a macrocosmic sphere that surrounds everything that happens in time. In this sphere everything lies inside each other, interpenetrating each other, not in chaos, but in an arrangement in which time is still pictured, indeed even actually exists, not as 'one thing after the other' but 'simultaneously'. The fruits of earthly experience appear along with purely spiritual experiences.

How can we imagine then the existence of this being, that bore the name Rudolf Steiner as spiritual scientist?

'Only' with pure thinking and a strong imagination can we already envisage what can be observed there.

We find there a being that is neither man nor woman, for gender is an earthly feature and only works in what is earthly. A being that has a strong relationship, even resemblance, with the cosmic intelligence. It is not a god, it is a human being, the human form of cosmic intelligence. One of the fruits of this being's last incarnation is the self-consciousness of intelligence: the being is completely self-conscious – as human beings can be now only in the physi-

164

cal body - because it has learned to know it in itself without the physical body, indeed even without an etheric foundation. Thus it knows of the human intelligence, and because this is the greatest concern of Michael, it is together with Michael, though independent. It lives in that world which it had already acknowledged on earth in its spiritual scientific research. The self-conscious knowledge therefore has to be present in the spiritual world.

But this being also carries the fruits of its former worldly incarnations. It seems to be similar to the whole world of Greek philosophy as well as to the Scholasticism of the Middle Ages. In the spiritual world it then experienced how the true being of this knowledge on earth steadily disappeared, how it went its own way. Now again it has to experience something similar. Anthroposophy which has been led down to earth separates itself from the original living source.

This whole being has also lived a sort of biography in the spiritual world. The fruit, the quality of the last incarnation is added to this experience. This 'biography' contains the following great experiences: the spiritual individuality had experienced how Christ entered the worldly world. It had seen Him departing, had experienced from 'up above' the life of Christ and his death and resurrection. The world-word, with which the individuality is connected so strongly through its relationship to human intelligence, left the spiritual world. One can clearly understand how strongly the desire of this individuality was to follow Him. To give himself to Christ's intervention. Is it not then very clear that the next incarnations all stand under the sign of Christ? In the spiritual world this individuality had to observe with great pain how the Athenian Academy was closed and how non-christian philosophers moved to Gondhishapur, when they tried to accelerate the scientific abilities of man. He has to observe how then a dogma is decreed by the Catholic church (869 AD), in which just this part of man, that relates to the growing individual intelligence, *the spirit*, is stated not to exist, and how he later, as saintly philosopher, still submits to this dogma, to then take up the impulse again in the spiritual world in order to represent the spirit on earth in his next incarnation?

However, one has to want to free oneself from one's own limitations, in order to be able to sense how *great* this individuality in the spiritual world is. It seems to be a kind of primal image of the human spirit. Thus not a God, but a pure human spirit, as it was meant to be by God, appears in all the incarnations of this individuality and shows the development of the spirit to the most truth-filled and most perfect form. It is not an ‚all-in-one-being‘, but an individual, with a task that embraces the well-being of mankind and shows a deep similarity to the being of the human spirit itself, the intelligence, how it was divinely intended to be.

When, so many years after Rudolf Steiner's death, we now want to think about him, we must dare to see him as much greater than he was as Rudolf Steiner. For he is no longer Rudolf Steiner anymore, not a man, not a woman.[66] He is the being, that has to save the human intelligence and keep it for the gods.

Let us turn now to this struggle.

---

[66] I don't consider the possibility here that this individuality could have returned to earth already. I know about four people who are alive now and who see them selves as the reincarnation of Rudolf Steiner. A fifth may not think it of himself, but is as regarded as such by others. Rudolf Steiner himself gave positive answers to questions about an early reincarnation. Nevertheless, I prefer not to consider it as long as it is not absolutely sure that he is here again.

The threat against human intelligence

In the past century we have seen the furious pace of development in the field of scientific and technical intelligence, and the pace has been growing ever more furious. 'Artificial intelligence' has become a medium discovered by man but one that powerfully surpasses human intelligence. The development of nuclear fission is something similar. It has a 'will-nature' that is discovered by intelligence but that also surpasses human intelligence tremendously. Technology destroys ecological balance; one discovers measures in order artificially to maintain this balance, but the measures themselves have consequences, for example meteorological effects, which one can control just as little. It is thus becoming clear that human intelligence outpaces what is human. What does this mean?

It was a divine intention that the cosmic intelligence be reflected in the human spirit. Man was not supposed to be overwhelmed by it, but have the capacity to gain control of it himself, while receiving cosmic thoughts as 'clear' thoughts of reason and learning, to be able to enter into them totally. But if God has become invisible, one can also *not* believe in Him. From this God-given freedom materialism originates. And on the field of intelligence that only wants to accept what is sensory, intelligence can be used by beings that desire it and want it for themselves. These beings can embody their own craving in the medium, in the 'matter', of human intelligence. And because they have a much higher level of development than man – one can also say lower – they can achieve in this medium what man on his own could never have achieved.

Just as a human being such as Rudolf Steiner has placed

his intelligence at the disposal of the divine beings – and that can only be done in freedom, out of one's own will - so a human being who is not living in self-conscious knowledge puts his intelligence at the disposal of the ahrimanic beings (led by the prince of this world, the master of death, or Satan). That happens as a matter of course; such beings invade one's consciousness and *only* flee from an intelligence that knows itself. These beings need the intelligence of human beings, which they occupy in a brilliant form. Human beings are proud of doing so and want more than they would usually have been able to achieve. Of course, these ahrimanic beings do not want to let man think anything that has any connection to the divine or any connection to pure human intelligence. They align themselves sharply and violently against the development of pure thinking, because this is their great enemy. Thus artificial intelligence, nuclear technology, environmental technology, but also orthodox medicine, and politics are all servants of these beings. The regent of intelligence, the Michael-power, has itself overcome these beings – exemplified in the figure of the dragon – already long ago. But first, man has to gain insight and for the sake of his freedom, he cannot do that through divine inspiration.

Human beings must spread this insight themselves. Such a human being was Rudolf Steiner. He lived before the process of artificial intelligence really got going. What is he doing today?

The effectiveness of Rudolf Steiner's individuality today[67]

In order to be able to experience the activity of this man, at that time and nowadays, a picture of his being has to be painted that was not mentioned before. Actually, it is not possible to express in words, because words are always connected to material existence, even when they are employed to describe the spirit. The characteristic of the individuality which is being sought here is a common human one yet is nevertheless very individual. It cannot be named in terms of content; there is no 'what'. But there is also no 'how', because actually, there is really no way in which this characteristic expresses itself. 'That' would be the right indication; it all points towards realizing '*that* it is active'. This characteristic exists only when it is realized. When this does not happen, it makes no sense at all to say anything about it. But when it is not named, the individuality of Rudolf Steiner is not at all correctly understood.

Thus, in order to get an idea of the activity of this primal image of intelligence, of the consciously self-aware intelligence, we must try to understand his being, his essence again, now in relation to this 'that', which seeks to express itself in the word 'love', an often-used but rarely grasped concept. If we want to understand what 'love' is, we can not bind it in content; it does not let itself be described as a 'something'. But neither is the 'how' enough. Naturally, one can cite many examples that show how much Rudolf

---

[67]   If this individuality is on earth again, his spiritual being will still do what is described here.

Steiner was a loving personality.[68] Woldemar Sacks tells:

> 'But more than all conversations the true great man was revealed to me by a small event. When one night we were debating with each other again, the unforgotten poet and eternal bohemian Peter Hille sat with us and ordered a cup of coffee from the waiter. Because we all knew that Hille never had any money, we wondered how he would rescue himself from this situation, because it was not possible to pay 'on account' in this café. Nevertheless, he called out when about to leave: 'Waiter, bill!' The waiter came and said: 'The coffee has been paid for!' After that, Peter Hille said to us, touched: 'Do angels fly around here? Which of you was it?' Now I certainly was not the one, and Steiner swore that he was happy that he was able to pay for his own coffee. And as there was no-one else in the café, Peter Hille left, shaking his head.
>
> When Steiner and I left the café in the early morning, he said resignedly (at that time he lived outside Berlin): 'Today I have to go on foot – not enough for the tram!' Of course I was too poor to be able to help Steiner, but – I offered myself as his companion. After we had been talking while walking through the night for half an hour, he suddenly said to me: 'You see, Saxerl, how good it was that I played the angel for Hille – would we have had this fine night walk otherwise?' However small this event may seem – it shows the great character of the man who would later be the spiritual representative of mankind.'

There are many more stories like that, one more of which I would like to quote here:[69]

---

[68]   *Der andere Rudolf Steiner, Augenzeugenberichte, Interviews, Karikaturen* (Accounts from Contemporaries, Interviews, Caricatures), Pforte Verlag, Dornach 2005, p.118

[69]   *Rudolf Steiner in Nederland*, 8, Leen Mees, De Jas.

'It happened in Hilversum, at the entrance of the room where Ru-
dolf Steiner was to give a lecture. It was organised by Mr. Kraan,
who I myself (being from Hilversum) already knew as a very warm,
quiet person.

Among the people who came in was a man who was wearing a long
coat. Kraan stopped him and asked him to leave his coat in the
cloakroom. Then the man said that he could not do that, because
he was only wearing a shirt underneath his coat and did not own a
jacket. Mr. Kraan answered that he was very sorry, but that he real-
ly could not make an exception in this case. 'I have my instructions'
he said, apologizing. Behind him stood Steiner, who very quietly
said to Mr. Kraan: 'I would let this man in nevertheless, because if
you do not let him in, I will not give my lecture.'

The ability to love is purely spiritual, and therefore so
hard to grasp. Only by 'encircling movements' is the goal
of understanding somehow reachable.

There is no-one who does not know love. Even the greatest criminal – at least in our time, maybe it will change in
the future – has a spark of love inside him, or longs for it. If
this spark is instigated, truly miracles can happen.[70]

The Dutch comedian Toon Hermans filled his stage work
with, among other things, the striving to let his audiences
experience something of love. He made it manifest through
his powerful performances, but also tried to approach love,
that everyone knows, through descriptive paraphrases:[71]

---

[70]   Mieke Mosmuller, *Inferno*, 2007; German edition of this novel, 2008

[71]   Toon Hermans & Mieke Mosmuller, *Gewoon God* (Just God), Baarn, 1998

If there were no love,
The rivers would stand still,
And the birds and animals too
If there were no love.
If there were no love,
The shore would leave the sea.
They'd have no more to say to each other
If there were no love.

If there were no love,
The moon would cease to shine,
And poets would cease to write,
If there were no love,
There would be no flowers anywhere,
The earth would lose its colours,
Everywhere closed doors only –
And the bells would no longer ring...

He also tried to help people experience that the all-embracing love for a loved one can extend to love for the created world. That one can *live* in love for the whole of creation and can experience oneself in this experience of a beyond. He did that when he sang not 'I love springtime…', but 'I springtime you'.

He taught the love of daily life, like a Zen-Buddhist can teach it.

In the individuality of Rudolf Steiner we find an intensification of this ability for love. Intelligence has three faces. We may be gifted with a shining, beautiful, enthusiast but arrogant intelligence. It comes from that light bearer that projects everything beautiful and intelligent as its own capacity. This intelligence is luciferic. I did not have *that alone* in mind in describing the primal image of intelligence. The second face comes from the previously described ahrimanic beings (they do not belong to the light, but are support-

172

ers of darkness). There is nothing artistic about this intelligence; it only provides quick analysis and combination, a lightning ability for insight, without an idea how this insight came about or what it is based on. The luciferic intelligence lives in thinking in itself, in having thoughts; the ahrimanic intelligence expresses itself fully on the basis of external, sensory observation.

Rudolf Steiner has balanced this polarity by a third form of intelligence. This intelligence is the purely human intelligence as it was meant to be by the gods for mankind. When the observation of thinking is realised man goes 'through the middle' between Scylla and Charybdis. This third form of intelligence is that with which man finds his way in the company of the michaelic power.[72]

> 'Now Benedictus could easily show professor Capesius:
> In lonely thinking lies the luciferic temptation again; in mere listening, mere observation lies the ahrimanic element. But one can hold to a middle condition, one can go in between, so to speak. One needs to remain neither in the pure abstract, brooding thinking, with which one locks oneself up as a hermit in the soul, nor to give oneself completely to pure listening and observing what the eyes and ears are able to observe. One can do something else besides these, when one makes what one thinks so lively, so strong, that one has one's own thoughts in front of himself as something lively, and enters into them as into something that one hears or sees externally, so that one's own thought becomes as concrete as what one hears and sees. This is a middle condition. In the mere thoughts that underlie brooding lies the approaching of man by Lucifer; in pure listening, be it by observing or by paying heed to human authorities, lies the ahrimanic element. If one internally strengthens oneself and wak-

---

72   Rudolf Steiner, *The Secrets of the Threshhold*, GA 147, p.98f.

ens the soul so that one, as it were, hears and sees one's thoughts, then one has meditation. Meditating is a middle condition. It is neither thinking nor observing. It is a thinking that lives with the same liveliness in the soul as observing lives, and it is an observation that has nothing external to it but rather, has thoughts as its object. Between the luciferic element of thoughts and the ahrimanic element of observation the soul life flows into meditation as in the divine-spiritual element that carries only the procession of the world-phenomena. The meditating man who lives in his thoughts so that they become as alive inside him as observations are lives in a divine in-streaming. On the right he has mere thoughts; on the left he has the ahrimanic element, mere listening; and he rules out neither the one nor the other, but knows that he lives in a threefoldness, that number orders life. And he knows that a polarity, a contradiction is present, a contradiction between two things, between which a balance has to be held in his meditating, between the luciferic and the ahrimanic element.'

Towards all that comes love. We find harmonious, observed thinking already in the first part of 'The Philosophy of freedom'. Love appears in the second part, where it is not directly described but *appears*.

We must take our point of departure from daily life. Earthly life is the school of love. It is not only a feeling, it is no thought. It is a deed through and through. How so? We mainly know love because we can love a special person, who becomes our life companion, for life. Let us leave all the flaws and mistakes out of consideration. This love exists for a certain man or woman. If it is love, which stays with us through all the storms of life, 'for better and worse', it is not only a thought or a feeling. It has the power, to provide endurance, devotion, patience, perseverance. That is will, that is deed.

One cannot possibly name it, this love. It is an unobservable power, which can work wonders. It points to the sacrifice of selfishness, but in connection to self-knowledge given by the loved one: the other gives you self-esteem, which one gives to others again. In true love one does not feel oneself, but the other. Through this, the other experiences who he is, and vice-versa. This releases the power that makes it possible, through the living together, to overcome all the difficulties that occur in life.

This must now spread to other people, to all people, the whole of creation, every plant, every stone, every animal... Self-knowledge must be sacrificed for the other, who then fills one with the blessedness of the other's existence. This is no idolising, but an ongoing occurrence, a permanent state of being active. The actual experience of the existence of the other provides the idea for a deed in the sense world, a moral intuition. The same love that lived in the experience of the existence of the other, now becomes a deed that is loved for its own sake.

That is the second part of the 'Philosophy of freedom'.

Now something occurs in human development that in a completely fulfilled form, totally steeped in it, allows love as deed to be experienced. Only the man who works his way up to understanding and activity can attain an experience of such an event in its full reality. This event is 'Christianity as mystical fact', it is the deed of the son of God, to pour Himself fully into a human being, to give Himself totally to him, to be able to go through death and be reborn as the spirit of the earth. This spirit, the Christ spirit, does not only, after its death, penetrate the human body, but the whole earth-body. Novalis expresses it in the following poetic lines:

175

'How, moved only through His love,
He has fully given us Himself,
And laid himself in earth
As the foundation stone of a godly city.'

In these phrases love allows itself to be experienced as an event.

Then the spiritual scientist took another step and reached a new level. This love, which through God's deed of love, was given to us as a capacity to be developed, now had to flow into the already obtained capacity for self-observing thinking, self-cognizing thinking. The spiritual scientist had to bring the love that represents self sacrifice, in which it changes the self into the other, into knowing. It is there where 'Michael leads to Christ'.

The saintly philosopher already had this love. There are stories about him that show how he was capable of this sacrifice of self-feeling:[73]

'In Bologna while he walks through the cloister to meditate, he comes across a brother from another monastery, who he does not know. The Prior had given this brother the permission to go to the city with the first brother that he would meet. 'Worthy brother', he said to Thomas, 'The Prior has said that you have to come with me.' Master Thomas Aquinas followed the brother immediately, accompanied him on his walk and let him reprimand him when he did not hurry enough. He was not as fast in walking as in obeying, because of which, in his words, 'the religious life is perfected, because man is subject to another man for God's sake, as God obeyed

73 Jacques Maritain, *Thomas van Aquino, en zijn betekenis voor onze tijd.* (Thomas Aquinas and his importance for our time.)

176

man for man's sake.'

...

'He preferred to appear naïve than simply believe in evil: the perfec-
tion of the understanding is in any case not damaged by an error in
matters of relative import. When a father in a cheerful mood calls
for him at the window with the words: 'Brother Thomas, come and
take a look, an ox is flying by,' brother Thomas walks to the window,
but the other starts laughing. 'It is better', says the holy man to him,
'to believe that an ox can fly, than to think that a monk can lie.'

The young knight, who wanted to get the dog Gardevias
for his love so that she could read the star writing, and who
then died for that, had the same willingness for sacrifice.

The love of this individuality must have been set on fire
when it looked down from the spiritual world to the earth
and saw the greatest deed of love that has ever existed: the
incarnation, suffering, death and resurrection of Christ.

We experience this love-ability by observing the saintly
philosopher, how he kneels in front of the cross, encounters Christ and after that, declares his whole intellectual
work to have been but straw. One must come to terms with
this devotion deeply, try to experience it, want to follow it,
cultivate it in oneself. Only when we feel totally permeated by it, will the possibility exist to understand Rudolf
Steiner's capacity for love.

He was human; one should not want to see him as in-
fallible. He was pure, and holy, but he walked the earth,
and feet have to be washed, even if someone is completely
pure. It does not make sense to look for mistakes with a
magnifying glass – because one would truly need one then.
The Master of the Occident said himself that they would
certainly be found. I am sure myself that one can not easily

find them; one is more likely to find statements that are not in keeping with modern 'trends', statements to which one can take exception. But is something not true if it is offensive? Are things only allowed to be said that are not offensive? Then the whole world should mantle itself in deep silence, because these days almost everything said is offensive ... and what is said is most often not even true.

But he was saintly and had an ability for knowledge that was consecrated, in which love streamed in. In printed reproductions of his lectures which contain only summaries of the spoken, one cannot observe this very well. But when the whole spoken word is experienced from a lecture that has been properly stenographed, one encounters his love in knowing. As one can feel the love in one of Novalis' spiritual songs (which expresses the love for Christ), in Rudolf Steiner's lectures one can experience the love for Christ that has become fact in a man. This deep inwardness does not signify thoughts or feelings but things that have happened, something that has really happened during the speaking. If one could have been present, as a listener, it must have worked marvellously, in a deeply touching way, changing the whole soul. While reading the lectures, there remains a delicate feeling, which, however, is very instructive. It teaches the reader the necessary devotion in turning to the spiritual world, the right respect that must keep the balance with such greatly increasing knowledge. This happening in the soul is love.

With this love, which is deed, Rudolf Steiner dissolved the Anthroposophical Society and founded it again during the 'Christmas Conference'. He gave himself to it lovingly as its spiritual leader. His spirit-soul was the bearer of the esoteric stream that he gave in love to the General Anthroposophical Society.

When he died, then, he had to draw back this esoteric stream from it and direct it into the spiritual world, because he himself was it, in a certain sense. The Society died with him.

But how has he worked on after his death? His spiritual friend Ita Wegman strongly believed that he would have still been connected to the Society if the members would try to experience him as a living, real teacher. His wife Marie Steiner had a different opinion. She wanted to aim at the purification of the soul in humility, in order to make herself worthy to experience the teacher. As always with such different opinions, both are right, and the truth lies in the middle.

We know that after death, the etheric body dissolves into the world ether. But we also know that certain etheric bodies, of initiated or great spirits, such as that of Goethe, for example, remain preserved, that they are images existing in themselves. They are like books, in which the human wisdom that has been gathered is stored. One living on earth can learn to 'read' in these books, which is easier than, for example, reading in the Akasha chronicle.

With the physical body one is not able to read in these books. The intellect that is connected to the physical brain does not even experience the existence of these etheric books. But neither can the cultured anthoposopher read in them. He reads the anthroposophical thoughts that have developed on earth but reads them with the help of his brain and therefore has only the intellectual content. Not even with pure thinking can one read them. Pure thinking admittedly has released itself from bondage to the senses but it does not yet think 'brainfree'.

But if one has developed so far that all the contents of

one's thinking – thus also all the contents of pure thinking – are removed from thinking and yet there is still a thinking that is both power and movement, *then* there is a possibility to read such books. That might not become clear to the meditating person in the beginning. But when he takes in the content of spiritual science in this 'medium', they change into moving life, the content becomes richer, livelier, more perfect. It becomes a reality that can teach. One reads in the thought-body of the individuality that was Rudolf Steiner.

But then the thoughts from the work of Rudolf Steiner are changed, because the thought-body itself is in development. It does not stay rigidly the same like a corpse or even fall apart; it grows, metamorphoses itself. It is in interaction with the etheric environment. One finds the Philosophy of Freedom again there, in a different configuration. In the current anthroposophical world there are many people who think that one cannot base oneself completely on the statements of Rudolf Steiner anymore nowadays, because the times are totally different now. With their understanding that has not developed any further they try to give anthroposophy a 'new face'. In a deeper sense they are right: anthroposophy has to change its configuration; it has to develop with time. But the understanding that is connected to the brain is never able to do so. It is precisely this that has to develop itself, so that man learns to read anthroposophy in the living etheric body. There he finds anthroposophy changed. There he finds a lively understanding of the soul, the spirit, the phantom, an understanding of the path of knowing itself, in the way it can be taken now.

Who truly loves this philosopher, this philosopher-saint, this spiritual scientist, this messenger of Christ, also has a connection to his soul. This connection is something very intimate, and it is fitting to speak about it only hesitantly. But it has to be spoken about, because we need this connection.

Who needs help in his life or in his task in the world can turn to Christ in question. In the Gospel of John (John 14: 12-14) we find this stated the clearest:

> *'Truly, truly I tell you: he who believes in me will also do the work that I do and shall do more than that, because I go to the Father. And whatever you shall ask in my name, I shall do that, so that the Father may be glorified in the son. Anything you ask in my name, that I shall do.'*

The spiritual scientist (the Rudolf Steiner individuality) is not a god; he cannot work in this way – regardless to which level he has risen. We can however turn to him and ask questions. He can give us *insights*; we can get advice in knowledge. This is how the relation to his soul works. Therefore, we must first raise ourselves to pure thinking. We must try to bring our *way* of pure thinking to resemble the work of Rudolf Steiner in a certain sense. Thus, one must enter into pure thinking in *his* way. From there one must *observe* one's own questions, and in the moment of observing, the answer is already thought inside us. If this does not happen, the attempt has failed. If we search further nevertheless, we come back to our own thoughts, and the answer will be our own answer.

We can turn to him as to a friend, and also if we need advice for our own life. But then the specific nature of this soul becomes clear to us. Because what always comes back to us is: Have no fear! No anxiety! It seems to be an existential characteristic of this soul, the power to overcome all fear and anxiety, the power that is connected with trust in one's own karma. These encouragements are not only of a mental kind, such as encouragement from one of one's fellows. They truly *work*, and thanks to them, one can better endure difficulties in life, one knows better how to relate to them. We can give Christ the trust that He can truly change our karma. The spiritual scientist gives living working advice.

We can also ask about our relationships with fellow human beings. Then we get to know a second aspect of this soul. The answers always come at once when we observe our own questions, and they happen to us completely naturally. We would never have given such answers ourselves; we *have* never given them. And when their content seems to be the same over and over again, it *works* variously every time, different, differentiated. The answers always indicate sympathy with others, the pity, compassion and joy.

But one cannot not imagine this too simply. I have been blamed for lacking compassion in my book against Judith von Halle.[74] In this book I did not attack Judith von Halle as a person. She is responsible for herself; I have not interfered in her life or activity at any time. But if one operates in public, the public will engage with one's statements with their own capacity for judgment. The spoken and written words of public figures must be tested for their truth; otherwise, we are only obedient slaves. With Judith von Halle there was the difficulty that she herself has connected her statements to her personality (her body), through which her statements are not free. It is precisely *this* that should be the point of departure for any criticism in her case. Thus

---

74   Mieke Mosmuller, *Stigmata und Geist-Erkenntnis, Judith von Halle versus Rudolf Steiner* (Stigmata and Spiritual Knowledge - Judith von Halle versus Rudolf Steiner), Occident 2008

in my judgment of Judith von Halle's statements it is not a question of compassion or no compassion. To have felt compassion would have meant that I would have felt that I had raised myself up above her, but the battle takes place *beyond* the soul realm; it is a spiritual battle, a battle for the truth.

Compassion belongs to the sympathies of the soul, to sympathy with the soul-waves of others. One does not have compassion for wrong insights. But one needs it when another has strong soul experiences, of a mostly personal nature: if one cannot feel compassion, the other stands there alone, completely alone with his feelings. Compassion releases the other from suffering; shared joy makes the joy stronger.

'Shared suffering is half the suffering', but shared joy is truly doubled, tripled, greatly multiplied.

The soul of the spiritual scientist gives these answers without moralising, as it might sound like I am doing here. One obtains them directly as one's own insights, and one's own morality never moralises.

Beyond that, however, true soul insights do exist, which one can create here.

In the mysteries of Ephesus the spiritual scientist had already obtained and used knowledge of the wandering stars. He knew how the powers of these wandering stars manifest materially on earth in the form of the metals. The soul world is, actually, the same as that of the wandering stars. The soul in its various members (astral body, sentient soul, mind soul, consciousness soul) belongs to this world, which bears at the same time also characteristic soul features, which relate with the nature of the metals.

In his collaboration with his spiritual friend, Ita Wegman,

this knowledge of the wandering stars and the relation to the metals still had to be renewed; it was to have become the theme of a second medical book, but the spiritual scientist died before this could be realised. The insights, however, are part of his soul being, and one can, through one's relation to this, expand one's own insights in this area, which before were only intellectual, into insights of a soul-spiritual nature.

In one of the last lecture cycles, 'Initiate consciousness'[75] one can get a foretaste of these insights, which signify a consequential effect and transformation of the mystery knowledge of Ephesus. Here the planetary beings, embodied in the earthly metals, are described as levels of the spiritual development, in association with the position of the 'Lotus Flowers' (chakras). The macrocosmic human being is spread out in the cosmos, the heart appearing with the sun, the head with Saturn and further up to the fixed stars, the reproductive organs with the moon, the feet on the earth. The cosmic Sophia appears, and one gets a sense of the actual anthroposophia. That is the human form spread out in space.

But there also exists a temporal dimension to these planetary forces, which the spiritual scientist gave in the lecture series 'The Easter Festival as a Chapter in The Mystery Wisdom of Man'[76]. There he brings the soul world in connection with the descent of the spirit and soul to earth, whereby the soul adapts itself to the planetary forces, outlined in the verse:

[75] Rudolf Steiner, *Initiate Consciousness*, GA 243

[76] Rudolf Steiner, *Mystery Centres of the Middle Ages, Rosicrucianism and Modern Initiation*, GA 233a

Offspring of worlds!, you form of light,
And by the Sun empowered in the Moon's full might;

Endowed with Mars' creative sounding
And Mercury's mobile movement;

Illumined by Jupiter's radiant wisdom
And Venus' love-born gift of beauty

So that Saturn's ancient spirit-devotion
May hallow for you the being of space and the becoming of time

Here the cosmic man is assigned to time, gives himself to the etheric and eventually also to the physical, when he assigns the planetary forces to his etheric body, which then, for example, 'guides' the physical design of the organs, but also the possibility to realize human qualities on earth.

It is not a repetition of the insights of Rudolf Steiner if one brings oneself into a true relation with the living spiritual scientist. It is like the difference between a forest of dried roses and a living, growing rose-tree. The difference is even sharper, because the rose always produces new roses, while living knowledge unexpectedly enables one to experience something new (as was already described above as 'bringing forth').

One does not have to be a clairvoyant at all. It is an intermediate level. A living, powered thinking must be present, and the ability to think further what one already has – in relation to the being of that individuality that in the last incarnation was called Rudolf Steiner.

The relation to the spirit of Rudolf Steiner

It is a bold desire to want to raise oneself to the spirit of the spiritual scientist, but it is justified. As Rudolf Steiner, he himself summoned his students to research his mystery name – an act which we are now practising and which is just what will raise us to his spirit. But here we do not want to get an impression of his being; we have already tried that. Now we want to search for a real relation to him.

The understanding of the spirit takes place through the knowledge level of intuition. This we naturally have only in the understanding of a concept. If we have developed pure thinking, we also have intuition in understanding thinking itself. With this intuitively grasped pure thinking we find the spirit of an individuality only when we search for a kind of summary of the spiritual action of the last incarnation.

Rudolf Steiner himself often stated that it was his task to bring forward a Christian 'doctrine' of reincarnation and karma. It is manifestly clear that he did bring this, and that it is actually working. If all the rest in anthroposophy is lifeless, the idea of reincarnation and karma lives, because it has been fully taken in by a great number of people into their views of life and death. Children who go to Waldorf Schools often have the completely 'natural' feeling that they have been on earth before and that they will also come back later. That is at least a beautiful fruit of the work of Rudolf Steiner. This is no longer 'just an idea'; it works through one's whole life and gives other, new possibilities that enable one to experience oneself and one's fellow man, and face them. Naturally, because of that, there has also arisen a new opportunity to criticise other people and to name certain diseases as the consequence of mistakes etc. But the fact is, that the idea has become effective.

This idea, however, represents the design of 'something' that is situated more deeply and that one can understand intuitively. The whole voluminous knowledge of spiritual science contracts this 'something' into a single concept, which thus also underlies reincarnation and karma:

'But the name (Anthroposophy) was chosen very well. And I adopted this name when I first had to proceed many times from the foundations that will be dealt with again in these lectures. Firstly: the sure spiritual fact for anyone who observes in the spiritual world, that there are repeated lives on earth.'

For this intuitively grasped 'something', one can choose the word 'development'; one only has to think it through as far as possible. Everything in the work of Rudolf Steiner points to development. If one studies his epistemological works in the right way, one has not only enriched one's being; one has become a different person, with an extended ability for knowledge. In the text of the 'Philosophy of Freedom' it is, for example, stated : 'I can *never* observe my present thinking, but I can only make the experiences that I have had in my thinking process into a subsequent object of thinking.'[77] After the right study of this freedom philosophy one has grown beyond it: one *can* then truly observe one's present thinking (and not only the experiences of it subsequently). That is the fruit of this study; one has developed oneself to the point where one can do that.

In 'Mysticism…' the development of the new sense is discussed; in 'Christianity as Mystical Fact' the fact of the development in itself is described. 'Knowledge of Higher Worlds - How Is It Achieved?' gives the path of develop-

---

[77]   Rudolf Steiner, *The Philosophy of Freedom*, GA 4

ment of the soul to the spirit. 'Occult Science – An Outline' enables the reader to experience how the earth is part of a grand developmental process, in which all participating beings develop further and further even if not all at the same pace. The mystery dramas show the development of individualities through a number of incarnations: the Christology lectures point to the being that has made a free, independent development possible at all: this being is development in itself.

'Death as Life Change' describes development further, and in 'Philosophy and Anthroposophy', the ideas of 'The Philosophy of Freedom' are extended. The threefolding of the social organism promotes development and finally, the 'Christmas Conference' set on a new course of development the rigidified Anthroposophical Society.

Now, the reader can extend this list indefinitely. The death of Rudolf Steiner then ought necessarily to be seen as the subsequent step in this development because otherwise, his own development and with that, the further development of anthroposophy, would be stopped.

But what is development?
The 'Panta Rhei' of ancient Heraclitus emerges here in a new form. Everything is in flux, everything is event, there only exists a standing still because new forces have to assemble in order for something to be able to occur. But a development is not *only* happening, it also has a content, a 'what' and a shape, a 'how'. Development lives in the moving on to higher and higher perfection and to ever new abilities and characteristics. And this living towards perfection and to the ever new must become even more perfect; it must come into being in ever new ways. For what is then the being of this development, of this happening? It is the

fully replete 'what', 'how' and 'that', it is love that is realised, made real.

In the pastoral-medical course Rudolf Steiner gives the following verse:[78]

> *'I shall walk the path*
> *That dissolves the elements in events*
> *And leads me down to the Father*
> *Who sends disease to regulate karma*
> *And leads me up to the spirit,*
> *Who leads the soul in error to gain its freedom.*
> *Christ Leads downwards and upwards,*
> *Harmoniously generating spirit-man in earthly man.'*

In rhythm, sound and effect one can experience 'something', a certain attitude, which the soul takes on when it speaks these words. It is the experience of a firm will that one wants to be faithful to, and a deep, relaxed calm that accepts the irregularities in development. In this soul attitude one can, if one rouses oneself to a powerful pure thinking, 'dissolve the elements in events'.

The mineral world does not itself know development. It only changes through outer influences. In flora development lies in the growing form and function of the changing parts of the plant. The ability for development rests on the correlation between sun and earth on the one hand, but is on the other hand also 'inherent'. The plant is always changing; it finishes by bearing fruit, and develops further, 'invisibly', to the next formation.

The animal has not only a 'developmental plan' of form

---

[78] Rudolf Steiner, *Pastoral-Medical Course, The Collaboration of the Doctor and the Priest*, GA 318

.

inside it, but also a soul instinct, a sum of instinctive characteristics that do not originate from the visible outer world.

Man carries part of his developmental ability inside him only insofar as it comes from the I.

Here the gate of development opens in the actual sense; an infinite perspective appears. Before the I was truly born, the development came from the divine-spiritual world (the countervailing powers included); after the birth of the I, this development partially turns around: man's I has to rule, through his own motivation, the soul, the etheric body and the physical body. The I-endowed human being takes development partially into his own hands.

The spiritual scientist showed us development in many forms; time and time again he directed attention to development. But development does not proceed in the same way in every human being. We already know that when we look at children's development. If this were not so, one would never let a child stay in the kindergarten a year longer. But that happens, and it is not a sign of negative criticism. Repeating classes in 'normal' schools has this negative connotation, but even there it is often beneficial to let certain abilities grow quietly, which can enable them to ripen in later life. Development goes on in different beings at different tempos, within the human race, indeed even between the divine hierarchies. It can go too fast or too slow. The right measure, the right tact, lies in the middle. Thus arises our many-layered creation, which is like a wonderful symphony. In a symphony too, not all tones are as outstanding as the others, but they are all important.

In the meditation of the washing of the feet[79], where one thanks all members of the creation, because one could not exist without them, one can permeate oneself with the right feeling for development. Development brings differences along with it, but there need be no value judgments. When we think of the threefolding of the social organism, differences between people only count in spiritual life; there one has to be able to distinguish the master from the student. But in legal life, on the contrary, there complete equality applies, and in economic life, brotherhood.

The spiritual scientist brought us the idea of development in the most extensive manner. It is the fundamental idea, the primal idea of anthroposophy. When we want to come into relationship with the spirit of the spiritual scientist, we must want to be filled completely with this idea. Otherwise, the spirit of this developmental scientist will eventually withdraw – and turn to individualities who are able, and inclined, to take up this primal idea of creation.

And how does one mainly take up this idea?
Through the energetic taking up of one's own inner development.

---

79   St. John's Gospel

FOURTH PART

The opponents of anthroposophy at the present time

Because I want to emphasise sharply the tragedy of this opposition, I shall comment on those opponents of anthroposophy who are *outside* the anthroposophical movement at the end, as external opposition does not seem to me to be so important. Much worse is the opposition among anthroposophers themselves, who turn *against anthroposophy* under an anthroposophical mask, as it were.

I know of three ways in which the attempt is made to paralyse anthroposophy. A fourth form comes from the 'outer' world.

The first form of inner opposition directs itself against the essential nature of the transformation of cognition from intellectual cognition to spiritual cognition.

I am not able to judge whether the men who represent this opposition are conscious of their own point of view (opposition to anthroposophy), or whether they are influenced unconsciously. There are at least two books in which this anti-philosophy of freedom comes to expression: 'Intuition und Ich-Erfahrung' (Intuition and the Experience of the I) by Renatus Ziegler and 'Beobachtung des Denkens' (The Observation of Thinking) by Michael Muschalle. Both books examine the challenging passage in the 'Philosophy of Freedom':[80]

'I can never observe my present thinking; I can only make the ex-

---

[80] See n.77, p.43

periences that I have had in my thinking process into a subsequent object of thinking.'

Renatus Ziegler finds the solution in a change of the meaning of the words 'observing thinking'. Observing, for Rudolf Steiner, is activity that has become substantive (subject), which means that he actually speaks about the observation of thinking (that could *never* happen at the same time). Ziegler makes an object, a 'something' out of 'observing: Observations come spontaneously as remembrances of past thinking that has already faded away. He postulates, on the basis of Steiner's word 'never', that an observing of the actual thinking would not be possible.

Muschalle points sharply to the word 'never' and the difference between the observation of thinking, and thinking through the experience that one can have about thinking afterwards.

What is the nature of the error that we have to deal with here?
It is remarkable to see how these philosophers mistake the word 'never' and immediately regard it with absolute seriousness. Do they also take the rest of anthroposophy as something literally and forever immutable?

'The Philosophy of Freedom' runs its course completely within intellectual thinking. Rudolf Steiner deliberately limited himself to this; he says so himself. In thinking, as the mind will allow, everything moves in time sequentially, one thing after another, not at the same time. Amongst other things, the mind is handicapped by being unable to think two things at the same time, thus it cannot observe thinking as it is thinking, because this would have to be done simultaneously; the observation would also have to

196

be thinking (because the mind *can* only think). It can not do it at the same time; it can *never* do that. It can make a thought more complicated, when studying or learning, and think it directly from memory. Thinking two things at the same time is not possible, is never possible. The mind must thus look back *after* thinking and from memory try to bring the experiences into consciousness, so that they can be made the objects of thinking, if one wants to take hold of this exceptional situation which is thinking about thinking.

In 'The Philosophy of Freedom' this impossibility is confirmed again by the image from Genesis, where the creating God can also only see what he has created after he has created it and sees that it is 'good'. If even God cannot do it, the 'never' (in Steiner's sentence above) is certainly appropriate.

Nevertheless, there is no 'never' here. It is the same strong negation that we also find with the image of the veiled Isis: 'No mortal has ever seen my face'. Novalis knew what had to be done: 'Then we must become immortal!' And this is exactly what we have to do, in order to overcome the word 'never'.

Did Rudolf Steiner already know at that time that it would become possible one day to observe one's current thinking? Or did he also have to wait until the time of his consciousness soul (35), until he was ready for that? What is certain is that he did unveil Isis, because in his later works he speaks clearly about the ability to observe thinking as it is happening.
And the *effect* of 'The Philosophy of Freedom' is precisely that subsequently, one has the ability, to think one's thinking as it happens. The person who *actively* realizes 'The

Philosophy of Freedom' in the right way can look at his current thinking after this realization. That is the essence of anthroposophy: the development of a seeing consciousness. The Philosophy of Freedom, as activity, goes beyond itself, because it raises itself to thinking with the etheric body, and there Isis is unveiled; there thinking sees itself directly.

Through the perpetuation of the idea that it is impossible to observe one's actual thinking as it happens, living anthroposophy is made impossible. Whoever trusts these men of intellect will find that his development rigidifies.

*

The second opposition is directed against development itself.

In our time there is a stream within anthroposophy that fully acknowledges the comprehensive meaning of the first stage of the development of the anthroposophical movement, which culminated in 'The Philosophy of Freedom', but denies the subsequent stages (the development of anthroposophy after the turn of the century). It sees the Christian colouration of Rudolf Steiner only as symbolic material adopted from tradition, which he employed in his time so as not to shock people too much. He therefore clothed his insights in a traditional garb.

If such had been the case, Rudolf Steiner would have been absolutely untruthful. Because while he would have known that a Christ in this sense had never existed, he nevertheless would have used these 'images' to express his insights – while all the time giving the impression that they were all true facts. Thus Steiner would have been untruthful, indeed actually a liar, because he would have presented images and described them as facts which he knew to be no existing realities.

These anthroposophers[81] have kept faith with Rudolf Steiner insofar as they hold his enlightenment in the 'I am' to be true. What came later, the whole differentiated spiritual science, can, according to them, be dispensed with as an elaborate inconvenience. Also, the hard work of meditation in order to achieve pure thinking and stages beyond, is an unnecessary strain, because enlightenment is an experience of 'I am', 'I am I', which enables one to realize that one is a projection, or protuberance, of the all-embracing human being. Everything worthwhile that one has achieved transfers after death to this HUMAN BE-ING as fruit; one individuality fades away, others originate through new projections... The becoming aware of this I am, which one can encounter even while engaging with the Internet, brings relief and great peace, because all men are ultimately equal, certainly different because of the different shapes of their particular projections, but the one not 'further' or less advanced than the other. Accordingly, there is always a need for collaboration and discourse, because two know more of MAN than one, although in enlightenment one can ultimately experience all in one.

Thus Christ can be discarded, because he was also a projection of MAN, an extremely extensive projection in Jesus, as this is possible for all men – Gronbach[82]: *'Jesus's ego was changed one hundred percent by the eternal and authentic Self. 'Not I, but Christ in me', says Paul. [...] In his double*

---

[81]   The Info3 Team: Sebastian Gronbach, Felix Hau, Jens Heisterkamp They base their ideas on Ken Wilber. In 2009 I published my counter to Ken Wilber: Mieke Mosmuller, *Arabeske*, (Occident).

[82]   Sebastian Gronbach, *Missionen* (Missions), p.192

name Jesus Christ represents a double message: the self-realizing IDEA. 'Christ' is a certain name of that IDEA. 'Jesus' is the name that stands for a man in whom and through whom the IDEA becomes present on earth.' And thus one has at last also released oneself from Rudolf Steiner, because what he knew through his illumination can only be less than what we, the currently illuminated, can know. In the meantime great fruits have been added to MAN...

Enlightenment in this way does what is morally necessary: the ego blows itself up until it explodes in the 'I am I'. 'I am I' knows that it is part of MAN, and acts accordingly.

Now it is a peculiar language which is speaking here. It is a half-serious language, but also a half-scientific one, full of mockery, conceit and presumptuousness, which lies hidden behind the mask of serious enlightenment.

This 'new anthroposophy' – that is fully congruous with other new-age illuminations – cannot be refuted. That could only be done with the spiritual science of anthroposophy, of Rudolf Steiner, the very knowledge that has been paralysed. Only the 'general' illumination from him counts as true in this ,new anthroposophy'; all the rest is just used as symbolic material, and thus not to be taken seriously. The statements that Rudolf Steiner made denying this equivalence of HUMAN values are all seen as points of view with regard to development, but mainly with regard to the *differences* between people; they are seen as discriminatory. Therefore it is understandable that from this group of anthroposophers the proposal for a memorandum came that was to be signed by as many anthroposophers as possible, who declared by their signatures that Rudolf Steiner had made discriminatory statements.

Thus one can no longer quote Rudolf Steiner in order to

correct defects and abuses in the form of anthroposophy today. Only he who has learned to laugh at himself heartily will still have the courage to do that – because it can no longer happen to him that he feels hurt when he is laughed at.

What are we actually facing in this New Age enlightenment – which has also been adopted elsewhere, by the Catholic church, for example ?

The true 'I am' that Rudolf Steiner found when he was a young man lies beyond pure thinking, beyond the stars. It really belongs to MAN, but to man who was created by the holy world-word, the cosmic word that has replicated itself in the manifoldness of the creation. This 'I am' is only reachable through an intense supra-physical, transcendental thinking. And it has a counter-image.

There is always a counter-image for that which is only attainable through strenuous renunciation; it is a counter-image which presents itself without effort. There is an 'anti-Father God', which was always called 'Ahriman' by Rudolf Steiner. He wants us to believe that the theory of evolution is true, even if it has a spiritual side. Then man is the most perfect animal in the animal species; this animal appears as a particular projection from the generic being MAN separately on earth, individualises itself there, but is, however, not a real, eternal individuality. MAN then, is just this anti-Father God, who scoops up everything received in the way of intelligence from subconscious, or semi-conscious, as it were, 'headless' thinking, and draws it into himself. All other true human virtues he does not appreciate; they can fall away. With this growing intelligence – stolen from man and then given back to man – he inspires the electro-magnetic (subsensible) field, where the world-wide web is spun, until the time when he can truly incarnate, when he becomes the 'anti-Son-of-God', the antichrist. The 'new' anthroposophy prepares his arrival on earth too, because it makes the weapons that it had through spiritual science ineffective. An ahrimanic darkening is experienced as illumination, as an 'anti-I am I', an absolute egoism with the appearance of selflessness.[83]

Whoever gets to know the living Rudolf Steiner knows that he has not dissolved into the universe at all, but that he is still present in his full humanity, perhaps he is even walking around in a physical body again and will show himself in the future.

The 'I am' experience of the young Rudolf Steiner thus grows in the course of years into an initiation in Christ. It is a widening of the thinking he had experienced to a spiritual experience of the whole man of spirit and soul (thinking, feeling and willing to the full extent of the I), that leads to an experience of the truly existing Christ. It is the highest, the most beautiful, the best thing that can happen to a human being – while the 'new anthroposophy', with false sympathy, mocks people who ask: how do I find Christ?

That is actually the only question that man must continuously ask, the only question in prayer. Those who want to get relief quickly and without strain do not put this question; they sit down in front of the computer, surf the internet… and become enlightened. These people acknowledge the spirituality of 'The Philosophy of Freedom'. They

---

[83] Here also I do not want to attack individuals, but the spiritual force they make visible and put in place of Rudolf Steiner's anthroposophy.

value the I-experience that Rudolf Steiner had when he was a young man. They see it as the enlightenment that was and is striven after in all spiritual streams, schools, mysteries: the all-in-one experience, that enables the union of all men to be experienced by a single HUMAN BEING. This enlightenment would lie beyond the cognitive levels of Imagination, Inspiration and perhaps even Intuition. All differentiation in plurality is held to belong to a lower level, and the entire spiritual science of Rudolf Steiner following this would thus be only an effort to find words for this enlightenment, find likenesses of it. Thus Christ would also only have been a human being, in whom this enlightenment was fully present, and Rudolf Steiner would have used him as an image because his listeners needed something familiar.

But Rudolf Steiner presented Christianity as a fact, not as an image. Thus, in doing so, he would actually have been a liar, a conjurer of images, who had complicated what is essentially simple. I repeat: according to the 'insights' of these men, Rudolf Steiner would be a liar, because in order to tranquillise people, so as to be able to communicate his experience, he presented something as fact, which actually was only was symbol.

In this idea of enlightenment there is only tolerance and frankness towards 'modern spirituality' in all its forms. Everything sounds wonderfully in harmony. At last the anthroposopher is released from his unpopularity; he can be lovingly enlightened together with everyone else. Development brings a kind of seclusion, and so one casts all this far away from oneself.

We have seen that the spiritual scientist himself is done away with. There remains something 'anthroposophical',

203

but Rudolf Steiner is equal to all others, indeed, he is even less than others, for we in our time have added so much to the HUMAN BEING! Would that not be development? No, it was only accumulation; it was not even growth. This 'enlightenment' does *not* lead to the unveiling of Isis, but to the darkness of subnature.

*

The third form of opposition is directed against what is Christian in anthroposophy in that it presents what is Christian only as *observations* (Judith von Halle).

Anthroposophy is spiritual science. It is science, and its organ of cognition as well as the object of its cognition is the spirit. It has brought knowledge of Christ that enables us to experience a spiritual (esoteric) Christianity, not only of a cosmic, but also a cosmic-earthly dimension. The Christ-spirit revealed itself in Jesus of Nazareth, connected itself to the Earth through death and resurrection and is now the spirit of the Earth and the spheres directly bordering on the Earth. One would always like to quote these wonderful sentences from Rudolf Steiner's mystery drama: *'Christ once lived on earth, and the consequence of this life was that in soul-form He envelops human becoming.'* Thus human development. We can obtain a scientifically exact understanding of the Christian fact through anthroposophy. We become able to share in the experience of this fact through our capacity for reason and not through statements of observations devoid of concepts.

If the anthroposopher is to believe in observations of which he cannot make any sense, he falls back into dogma. I have already said enough about the representative of this opposition in my book 'The Stigmata und Spiritual Knowledge'[84]. It is opposition because the essence of anthroposophy, namely, that it is *spiritual science*, is replaced in devious ways by an incomprehensible pseudo-science. Through the work of Judith von Halle, the credibility of Christian spiritual science is damaged and people who are seeking Christ are misled.

*

Then there is the fourth form of opposition, which comes from the non-anthroposophical world and has many faces.

In our contemporary world, which is determined by certain power principles, an effective philosophy of freedom is a threat to this power. Free individualities would not let themselves be frightened; they would stand up courageously and be what they want to be, and do what they think right and necessary. They would have the courage to go against public opinion because they would stand for truth, no matter what would happen as a result. Loss of position, loss of reputation, enduring incriminating judgments, mockery etc., - none of these would cause the free individuality, permeated with Christ, to give way.

Strong forces from the world are directed against a possible resurrection of the dead anthroposophy. The most effective way to do this is to attack Rudolf Steiner himself, because he can not defend himself. And one can strike him with something that in the mind of public opinion is the most disgraceful of all: the charge of discrimination

---

[84] Mieke Mosmuller, *Stigmata und Geist-Erkenntnis. Judith von Halle versus Rudolf Steiner* [Stigmata and Spiritual Cognition. Judith von Halle versus Rudolf Steiner]

or racism. Above all, since the second world war, in which an example was given of how far racial discrimination can go, discrimination is the worst a man can be accused of, because it clearly shows that the individual in question knows neither love nor integrity, that he must be a narrow-minded person etc. Now it is naturally the case that for the materialistic intellectual all words stand next to each other like stones, each worth as much as the other - what is said is said, what is written is written; and printed means recorded for ever.

The extensive 'collected works' of Rudolf Steiner (Gesamtausgabe) contains modern mystery knowledge. It was emphasised over and over again, that only one who has acquired a deep knowledge of anthroposophy can pass judgement on it. In the words of the spiritual scientist himself:

'It must simply be accepted that there will be mistakes in the drafts not verified by me. A judgment on the content of such a private printing can only be allowed to one who knows what constitute acceptable criteria for such judgment. And that, for most of these printed texts at least, is the anthroposophical understanding of man and the cosmos insofar as his being is described in anthroposophy, and what can be found as 'anthroposophical history' in the communications from the spiritual world.'(From 'The Course of My Life')

It is also clear that this mystery knowledge must not be thrown out into the street. It must for example not be taught to children, because they are far from ripe for it. I found it terrible to hear that our daughter had to hear in Religious Instruction in the 'Christian Community' about the incarnations that John the Baptist had lived through. That is absolutely *not supposed* to happen. But it does. There are other ways in which the science of the mysteries comes to people who do not at all want it. It is yet something else when a sceptic makes the effort to read a lecture cycle, or an anthroposophical book, or when several statements are simply repeated, taken out of context. Once that has happened, and seemingly incomprehensible passages from Rudolf Steiner's lecture work and books are made public, the hostile powers pick this up with pleasure and energetically start to battle against Steiner and anthroposophy.

Can the Pope be convinced that anthroposophy is purely Christian? Well, he probably knows it, but must oppose it anyway. An acknowledgment of the truth does not always mean that it can be acknowledged in public, or even be accepted. Can one convince an opponent of anthroposophy that Rudolf Steiner was not a racist, that he did not discriminate? That will never succeed, because the opponent does not *want* to be convinced. And then what? Well, then we try to make concessions to him, we concede a little here or there then he will be quiet and leave us alone. We raise the white flag and surrender to the prevailing judgment. What else? Must we let ourselves be judged as racists, because we are followers of Rudolf Steiner?

Concessions have never helped in such struggles. In the Netherlands it was openly admitted that there are many places here and there in Rudolf Steiner's work that are offensive, discriminating or even a criminal offence at the current time. Have the opponents held their tongues since then? Yes, but only because they have achieved their goal. For the whole Dutch nation Rudolf Steiner has been considered a racist since that time – in spite of the fact that it was admitted in publication that no actual racism was found! Rudolf Steiner is compromised, and that was the goal.

In 2008 something similar took place in Germany. Several anthroposophers themselves got down on their knees, admitting humbly in a memorandum, with as many signatures as possible, that yes, there do exist such questionable sentences and yes, we reject them. Consequently, Rudolf Steiner would also be publicly compromised in Germany. The opponents were given what they wanted, but fortunately, it has not amounted to much.

So what then? How should one deal with this?

When Rudolf Steiner was still alive, there was a slander circulating against him in the Anthroposophical Society. There was an accusation made by Dr. Goesch in 1915. Rudolf Steiner listened to it all and also how the members reacted to it. He then stood up and said: 'I wish to have nothing to do with such a Society!' And he left the room with his wife. Led by Michael Bauer, members sent him a written request for forgiveness, signed by many of them – and in response to this request, he forgave them and worked on as spiritual teacher.

The spiritual scientist also says 'I wish to have nothing to do with such a Society!' in his life after death; we should take it very seriously. If trust in the Master flows away and dissolves, he will no longer concern himself with his students. He does not need us; there are other people who rate his value and want to follow him. He does not need us, we need him.

The Path to Truthfulness

Truth is the most important condition on the path to the spiritual world and is already the realization of a part of this path. The truth is as soul configuration itself the start of a spiritually seeing consciousness. Without truth, there is no possibility to raise oneself to the spiritual world, and whoever consciously steps over the threshold of the spiritual world can do that because of his truthfulness.

By truthfulness I understand conduct that causes the being or the essentials of a situation to appear as completely as possible. The *condition* that then results could, in qualitative terms, be called 'beautiful'. The *process*, the conduct must qualitatively be called 'truthful'. Untruthful then, is conduct where something else lives inside the being than what is expressed outwardly. Man can be consciously untruthful and can also be unconsciously untruthful. Untruthfulness can even become second nature, a habit.

Nevertheless, not every form of truthfulness is the right one. There are three forms, and only one of them is the middle way. Truthfulness means conduct in which man keeps everything in the right balance.

In the life of instincts and desires one can be truthful. That is the truthfulness which is the characteristic of our time. One has his desires, his instinctive emotions, and expresses these without holding back. There is no interval between the instinct and the expression; the latter follows the former just like a reflex to the instinct or emotion. This conduct is called 'freedom', because one has the feeling that he does not have to be subject to rules, standards, and laws.

One is as truthful as the animals. I was present at a little discussion between two young people; a young fellow said: 'Man is simply a higher animal. I'm with Darwin; the evolutionary theory is scientifically proven.' A girl, one of the boy's friends, answered: 'You are right about that, because you just *want* to live like an animal!'

In the emotional life there is a second sort of truthfulness. If one fully identifies oneself with one's feelings, one is truthful. That is called 'subjective-emotional', for example; if one values it positively, it is called 'authentic'. 'Truthful' stands for the quality of the conduct seen from the viewpoint of the I. 'Authentic' points more to judgements made by others. When one thinks that a man acts the way that he really feels, one calls it authentic.

In this area of truthfulness one comes into that area of life where people say: 'there is no accounting for taste.' It is not only about taste, but also about opinions, which are based on feelings, and about certain types of modern art, where the artist embodies his subjective feeling directly into the work of art. He does not try to create a distance from his feelings, so that he would eventually be able to judge himself and others more objectively but he simply just puts himself into the world. This is not always wrong, but it can indeed be wrong. All unfairness stems from that.

One finds a third form of truthfulness in thinking, *if* it even exists. In thinking truthfulness is mostly not present. In order to make this clear, in what follows I shall look at thinking more closely.

One's daily thinking includes mostly subjective opinions and judgements, personal memories and beside that, all kinds of practical thoughts. Here thinking is actually not a thinking in itself, but thoughts of feeling and willing. Only in scientific thinking does the question of truthfulness arise in thinking. I do not mean the question about *truth* here, that is a different question. One can very well think the truth, and despite that not be truthful.

Truthfulness in thinking only appears when there is no distance between the thinker and the thought anymore. If this distance exists, then one has to deal with abstraction, or with untruthfulness (conscious or unconscious lies or errors). In thinking one is only truthful when one can fully see through the thought, and that is only the case when a man himself – with his whole humanity, with his whole thinker-being – can live in, and be present in, thinking.

Let us take, for example, the law of the circle. One can learn it by heart and say it out loud exactly right. The actual active man is then living in memory and in speech, not in thinking itself. Only when the rightness and validity of this law is thought is one present as thinker. That is also the case with complicated thoughts. With a good memory one can also say out loud the proof of Pythagoras' proposition, without a concept in one's head. That is abstraction. Only when one has completely grasped the proof can one truthfully think it through.

This is why the sin against the Holy Spirit is the most serious sin. This sin is committed when one denies a spiritual thought that one has nevertheless completely grasped, or even makes something totally different out of it. Thus, whoever does not have this truthfulness in his thinking cannot commit this sin against the Holy Spirit. With the awakening of truthfulness comes great responsibility. It is understandable therefore, that people recoil from that. In anthroposophy it is, however, a *fundamental condition,* characteristic

211

of its whole being. If one does not have it and does not want to develop it at all, anthroposophy is impossible, a contradiction of the deeper *willing*, which then actually is an unwillingness.

For what was always the main motive in the life of the philosopher, the philosopher-saint and the spiritual scientist? *If thinking and thought are one and the same, then the word is both the concept and an image of the spirit, from which it originates.* That same thing also applies to thinking about an external object, because there one also finds the spirit, only the direction is reversed. When the thinker thinks his own thinking, he has the concept of his own spirit. When he thinks of an external object and lets him*self* flow into it as thinker, he thinks the actual real spirit of the object. The removal of the distance between thinker and thought is the overcoming of all abstraction, and at the same time also the overcoming of the opposition between the I and the world.

That is the aim of anthroposophical meditation - that the thinker is nowhere else than in what is being thought and he pours himself out completely in thinking, that he becomes the thought himself, identifying with it completely. Therefore, the thought must be 'totally surveyable', which means that *nothing else* than the thinker himself enters into the thought, and not the personal self with all its opinions, judgements, memories. Only the *thinker, in as far as he is similar to the thought* may and must unite with it. In this way, pure will is led into pure thought. As a result, the thought does not remain just thought, but becomes real power, thought-power, which is willpower at the same time. *Then thinking and thought have become one and the same.* One has then awakened truthfulness.

How does this union of thinking and thoughts relate to the need to take in the 'exceptional state' that appears to signify precisely a separation of thinking and thinker?

Both activities – meditation and the 'observing thinking' of thinking – lead to exactly the same result: the unification of the thinker with his thoughts. Why?

In meditation one takes a thought chosen from the range of the thought life and unites oneself with that. The thinker thus puts himself 'beyond' daily thinking; he leaves it, as it were, in order to be able to consecrate himself to his higher work.
Will gradually streams through the thought and transforms itself into a supra-personal will. This is now not a blind will, like ordinary will; it becomes an eye, because the thought makes it see. Thus, the thinking force sees itself; it is present in seeing itself. The 'observing thinking' of thinking is awakened.

When, on the contrary, one proceeds more along the path of 'The Philosophy of Freedom', one comes to the same point by another route. Thought power is not developed here through the willed holding fast to a single thought, but through the constant effort to keep one's inner gaze on thinking. One thinks the thoughts of 'The Philosophy of Freedom', tries to realize them, tries to test them in one's own inner self. Through the enormous inner activity that one has to apply to that, because there has to be a continuous wrestling to hold on in the exceptional state, it finally succeeds: the will that has entered into thinking becomes eye. One can also say that thinking itself becomes eye, because both are one and the same – and yet different.

Thus the exceptional state is realized as an exception,

213

which is only possible in the spirit. The inner observer is awakened and he has the spiritual capacity not only to contrast himself with the physical-etheric, but also to observe *himself*. With this ability, he steps from meditation into daily life. This is only possible when he has learned to observe the spirit. Only then can he grasp his own will while seeing it. Everything that one does is then permeated by spirit. This capacity is love for action, and the capacity to see into the will with self-conscious thinking then leads to a consciousness of the eternal core of the being and of former incarnations.

That is anthroposophy.

Whoever has learned to live in this real anthroposophy cannot endure the situation in the Anthroposophical Society.

I must discuss another form of opposition against truthful anthroposophy here, and that is the internal opposition within the Society, within individuals themselves, who are very 'regular' anthroposophers. This opposition is disguised and constitutes a partially conscious and partially unconscious anti-anthroposophy. It manifests itself right up to the level of the Vorstand of the Society. That this is the case is clearly evident from the fact that several members of the Vorstand were the first to sign the discussion paper 'Claims of Racism against Rudolf Steiner - A Draft Memorandum', issued by Ramon Brüll and Jens Heisterkamp. Indeed later, the members of the Vorstand declared that their signatures related 'only to the procedure and the sought-after discussion', and not to the text of the draft itself. But they did sign it.

It is manifest untruthfulness, when Vorstand-members of the Society, which is supposed to serve anthroposophy, openly renounce trust in their founder.

By anti-anthroposophy I mean an untruthfulness in thinking, for this is not in any way consistent with true anthroposophy.

Untruthfulness itself starts where anthroposophy is 'treated' abstractly instead of unfolding itself truthfully from the inside out. Rudolf Steiner already pointed to the internal untruthfulness, which was perhaps the most clear in the 'pedagogical youth course'[85], but also on other occasions. Thinking anthroposophical truths must always stay connected to the inner human being and never separate itself from it. A mathematical sentence may be spoken out aloud without understanding of its concept, a spiritual scientific content never – otherwise one truly sins against truthfulness, against anthroposophy as a living, real being. Anthroposophical thoughts must never become phrases, behaviour based on thoughts should never become convention - *although there is a whole system of 'anthroposophical' conventions* - and actions, whatever they are, should never become routine.

Spiritual science also may not be thought with a deeper agnosticism, with an actual doubting of the truth or of the possibility of spiritual knowledge. This would also be an untruth because anthroposophy cannot be different from spiritual science and one must from the outset acknowledge the human capacity for spiritual knowledge. In order to mask doubt, relations in the Society are sentimentally glorified, and authority is simply assumed.

---

[85]   Rudolf Steiner, *Geistiger Wirkenskräfte im Zusammenleben von alter und junger Generation, Pädagogischer Jugendkurs* (Spiritually Active Forces in the Common Life of the Older and Younger Generations – Pedagogical Youth Course), GA 217

When the anthroposopher lives in a time like this, when serious spiritual science is so threatened, when anthroposophers do not educate themselves in truthfulness or do not even understand that they must seek it, the result can only be anti-anthroposophy, as we have already seen.

The result is a thought-content of anthroposophy that is only abstraction. Even if people are enthusiastic about it, that is not enough. Spiritual science stands there like a spiritless, groundless form of knowledge.

But one tries to make a case for spiritual science by means of conventional science, which is of course not possible. Release from abstraction only comes from argumentation based on the application of will in thinking through which the thoughts bear their reason *in them*. Abstract, spiritless knowing makes for dogmatism, for knowledge that one accepts without first having connected oneself completely to it with one's inmost being is dogmatic. Through that one is placed outside oneself, because it allows no possibility to test the knowledge in itself; it is seen from the outside. One looks at oneself from the outside and must judge from that external perspective whether dogmatic judgements and rules are being adhered to. A being is awakened that works outside the human being, as a judging authority. It becomes a kind of 'universal' that is held to be valid for everyone in the same way and to the same degree. This being goes around in the Society among people, influences them, and changes them. A group of people arises, who without knowing it, are prey to this being. Naturally, the question remains as to whether somewhere there is nevertheless someone – or more people – who brings this about deliberately.

One is so scared of the unfolding of self-interest that all

freedom only lives as a phrase. Beautiful words are heard everywhere but they work in a terrible way if one has ended up falling into the hands of this 'universal'. Anthroposophy must be 'universal'; what is personal must not. Christ is never to be found in a system of thoughts, not even when these have originally sprung from the spirit. We can only find Him when two opposite worlds are balanced, when our will has become one with our thoughts.

This fear of the personal is based on an aversion to truthfulness in impulse and feeling; one can understand that very well. A self-education in the anthroposophical sense means a transformation of the desire nature with its instincts and a transformation of the subjective-emotional element – a transformation, not an ignoring or a suppressing. Since these two forms of 'honesty' are feared, an honourable truthfulness is also regarded with suspicion, and everything that comes forward that is strongly connected to the will is basically rejected. One thus arrives at Ahriman, out of fear of Lucifer.

A truthful anthroposopher should not be ashamed of his egoism but acknowledge it courageously, and then conquer it, where it has to be conquered and develop it powerfully where it is in the right place: where the will must enter into thinking. The soul becomes pure, because the egoistic will must unfold itself in a selfless place: in thinking.

In anthroposophical circles it is regarded as 'improper' to talk about anthroposophy in a personal way. If one does that, one is said to be 'human all-too-human'.

This phrase is mostly used completely inappropriately, because it does not apply to personal or instinctive motives in general. Rudolf Steiner always used it when referring to the unconscious emergence of soul impulses that were acquired in former initiations but that are now dead places in the soul life which, if they run free unconsciously, change into desires. Thus without clairvoyance, one cannot at all determine whom one is dealing with when one encounters one's fellow man.

Now I belong to anthroposophical circles only insofar that I study the works of Rudolf Steiner and have subsequently tried to become a spiritual scientist. Beyond that, all my connection to anthroposophical circles ceases, because *living* the work of Rudolf Steiner leads to experiences that I have not been able to express *once* in such circles, either because I could not bring myself to say something – I have often been silent – or because a kind of anger approached me directly from others. So I do not stick to anthroposophical conventions; I have a completely different view of the concept 'personality'.[86]

When someone starts to engage in anthroposophy, he has nothing at his disposal at first except for his personality.

---

[86] This was written in 2008. In 2013 I travel through Europe to give seminars, and I speak openly about my vision of anthroposophy.

Love, too, can only be personal at first. If one discards one's personality before the spirit is truly born, one is given over to a bloodless, breathless, weak-willed group mind. To be oneself is then held to be the greatest sin. Thus, despite my aversion to his spiritual notions, I can very well imagine how a man like Sebastian Gronbach has torn open this shell, in which he was still trapped as an adult, and threw it away.

Thus there is at first nothing but the personality, with which one can experience anthroposophy as well as Rudolf Steiner himself if this experience is to be a *living* one.

But also later, when the spirit is truly born, one looks back with interest at the personality, because there, something is *experienced*, felt. Our personality must become part of the spirit, instead of our wanting to *overcome* it, which only leads to suppression. Such suppression leads to a Society of nothing but unreal people, who with their normal selves put themselves, as it were, outside themselves – they are forced to do that because they are continually judged by all kinds of anthroposophical criteria – and then are just led into a terrible self-obsessed attitude that kills all love. In love one forgets one's personality, with the risk that it becomes very, very visible…

I shall now describe my personal experience of Rudolf Steiner, and also of the spiritual teacher who is still present. If many people would reflect on this personal experience on their own, the spiritual form of this teacher would bloom in the spirit. But the opponents would be paralysed, because such an experience, multiplied, would work very powerfully.

Rudolf Steiner is a spiritual teacher who continuously summons one to act, and thereby actually summons one to love. But this love is not a sweet pseudo-holiness; it is risk, a hazardous undertaking in every respect. Rudolf Steiner has indeed left behind his whole library, from which one could draw the conclusion that it is only about knowledge. It does concern knowledge, but a knowledge that has become a *doing*.

I repeat once more that I do not worship the spiritual teacher as God; he is a human being. But he is a greatly developed man, fully permeated by Christ, which is why the words of Christ apply to his teaching (John 7, 16-18): *My doctrine is not mine but his that sent me. If any man will do his will, he shall know of the doctrine, whether it be of God, or whether I speak of myself.*

It does not make any sense, *only* to want to understand a thoroughly christian teaching, one needs to prepare oneself to implement His will; only then will one know if the teaching originates from God or from an ordinary man.

For me it was clear from the first sentence that I read of Rudolf Steiner's work: this is not only a task of knowledge; one has to want to change oneself, and in the work of Rudolf Steiner lie the threads that can guide that change. It has to be a striving for holiness, but in the full consciousness that this cannot be obtained just like that, but only on a long road. And the first task is then: only to keep busy with one's own holiness!

The spiritual scientist is thus a man of deeds, of love. That becomes very clear from what we know of him. The young Rudolf Steiner was very enthusiastic about his insights and brought them forward strongly and powerfully on paper and in conversations. In some of his lectures he is even said to have been 'intense'. He was very critical of Wagner's

221

music, saying that music should not have any pictorial or verbal content. He says himself that he did not enjoy having to admit later that he was mistaken in a certain way because he only later fully understood the music of Wagner. Thus Rudolf Steiner was no sanctimonious character, but an energetic, enthusiastic human being who wanted to enter fully into life with his whole personality – this was just his capacity for love.

But he was also no fanatic, because he possessed an all-embracing thinking, a completely unprejudiced mind, with which he could perceive every way of thinking and point of view. He was a highly gifted man, both in thinking and in his capacity for love.

Both of these qualities kept on growing; on the one hand they were brought to a state of calm, and on the other, they were shaped ever more livingly. He is the man who in our time achieved what is highest, loveliest, and finest in our time.

And he showed us a kind of hypomochlion in this development: a point of stillness, around which everything turns, a point that remains completely quiet, even when all relations change completely. Here lies that which was already present in the philosopher and which became christianised in the philosopher-saint. At this point man acknowledges that he is a being endowed with meaning, and at the same time it becomes clear to him that everything in the world is filled with meaning. This is the point at which the free human intelligence recognizes the divine. Here self- knowledge becomes world knowledge; world knowledge becomes self-knowledge. At this fulcrum point I have experienced the greatness of the spiritual scientist: man is sufficiently endowed to be able to come to this realization, but Rudolf Steiner makes him fully aware of it. When one is prepared to realize this himself, it is immediately clear, that 'the teaching of Rudolf Steiner comes from Christ and not from himself'.

Epistemology lies before this point; spiritual science lies after it. We find the living Rudolf Steiner at this unique fulcrum point, where the whole capacity for knowledge is acknowledged, where the human ability to experience meaning is widened around the object of the capacity for knowledge itself. That which is meaningful, activity filled with meaning is here understood – and that is the meaning of being human, the realization, the birth of the spirit, the point of departure for autonomous knowledge of the spirit.

The whole world appears to be filled with meaning, because we are no longer locked up in only our own 'meaning', but are able to look at ourselves from the outside.

I stood on the beach. The water flowed calmly to the beach, but there were swells, impulses in the water, incipient waves, now streaming there, meeting other waves, rolling over, rippling. I saw the will that drives the water, this wonderful undercurrent that causes the waves to arise, moves them forward, gives them all kinds of shapes.

This water of the sea is similar to the power of thinking, which also moves, is moved, makes shapes move. But it contains no meaning; it contains only will power. It is the power that is found and created by concentration and meditation.

One can experience further that these movements affect meaning, that they are connecting powers, powers that cause a concept to evolve out of the other, because both relate 'organically'. The flowing, moving, thinking power is the power of growth, but it brings forth meaning and is affected by meaning. Without meaning there would be no creation, because meaning sense is the connection, the harmony, the sounding, creating cosmic word.

That is the result, if one has the endurance for it, of doing what would be impossible according to the 'never' in *The Philosophy of Freedom*: always trying again, meaningfully observing cognition that seeks for meaning, now, in the moment. There we do not only find cognition, but also this man, who stands so close to the primal principle of knowing; this man, who once bore the name Rudolf Steiner.

And because every man has this primal principle inside him, we also find our own I, the spirit of individuality. This is no all-merged-in-one experience, but a strongly differentiated experience of the individual self. This experience has a powerful 'essence' that spans the whole biography and that can draw further circles, from its starting point to the periphery of the cosmos.

The teaching shows itself by its deeds to 'come from God', and what does that show about the teacher? What we achieve on a small scale, he has achieved on a large scale as knowledge that has become fact. Only in the *doing* of anthroposophy does one get an idea of the spiritual stature of Rudolf Steiner. How could one then ever want to judge this man, who is our 'predecessor' in development? That is completely impossible. One must leave the statements which one does not understand right where they are – and develop oneself more. The moment will come later when one can appreciate them. And if we are not even able to appreciate certain statements with all our anthroposophical knowledge, how should 'lay people' be able to appreciate them? In my view, it is a crime against the spiritual scientist to hand his statements, taken out of context, to the ignorant outside world, along with one's own lack of capacity for knowledge. The memory of Rudolf Steiner must be protected; *he* must be protected, instead of being cast like a pearl before swine.

He is still present, he is not dead. He can truly be active, if his students *realize* anthroposophy. That means so much more than employing his insights and the arts that he developed. It would mean that there would appear more and more individuals that are truly free, who would emanate warmth and understanding. Then public opinion would not doubt the goodness and the humanity of this spiritual teacher, because one would recognize the tree by its fruits.

One does not find the living Rudolf Steiner in quotes or anecdotes. It lives in the talent to understand the world as filled with meaning; the investigating and experiencing of this makes us feel the spirit in our self, stronger and stronger, until it differentiates into the spiritual world and condenses. That the human spirit is capable of this comes from the capacity to love which realizes itself, so *that* it can happen that the teaching becomes deed, through which the human spirit reveals its divine origins.

If anthroposophy is really to advance on Earth, it needs the return of this individuality who is so much further advanced than the rest of humanity in the development of spiritual powers of knowledge and spiritual love. The question must, however, arise: would it have a meaning if he were once again here? People living today must really ask themselves this question. And the answer would at the same time be an answer to the question: If he is reincarnated now, can he come forward?

The Consciousness Soul unfolds, and mankind has stepped unaware across the threshold of the spiritual world. This is a contradiction. It is clear, that we are very self-conscious. Even the man who feels little self-esteem is nevertheless mostly very self-aware. We live in the strong awareness that we mean something. It can be a meaning of physical beauty, it can be a meaning of intelligence, of the capacity for love, or whatever. Whatever it may be, it is always the body that provides these capacities. For beauty and intelligence we surely have to thank our body (although the body originates from the spirit, its creation is at present not to be attributed to our own input). The capacity for love is also mostly not soul-spiritual at all but is based on physical predisposition and education. Thus we have not yet developed a conscious soul at all that calmly knows what it is worth. Our self-consciousness is based on temporal values, on capacities which will fall away again when our body dies.

A characteristic of this self-consciousness is that it does not want to be told anything from outside. It knows, can and wants to do everything itself, only itself.

Precisely because it is only based on the physical, it does not have the ability – which is natural to the soul-spiritual pure consciousness soul – to step over the threshold of the spiritual world consciously. It was Rudolf Steiner who provided guidance for a conscious crossing into the spiritual world, and it was shaped on the basis of the development of a christianized, pure Consciousness Soul.

Only such a soul would be able to receive a 'new' Rudolf Steiner; only people who would have developed *this* would be able to understand that it was *him* who was on earth again. But this pure Consciousness Soul does not exist by itself; it must be developed in freedom. This development is, however, not within sight.

Up to now it is the Consciousness Soul that is bound to the body which has dominated our era. Man develops in such a way that the Consciousness Soul will be the basis for the war of all against all in later epochs – because the human soul can still only endure itself. Man not only does not endure insights that he receives from others: he has to have obtained them himself; he also cannot bear judgments from another human being and he cannot bear love from his fellow man, because that implies a lower position. The loved is the servant of the lover. Love gets the same treatment as compassion. The self-conscious person does not want compassion. Ultimately, he no longer wants to be loved.

Differences between people are not allowed anymore, and so it becomes harder and harder to look up to other people because they are more developed. Wiser, more intelligent, more loving, more tolerant, more frank, more positive...

Step by step, man loses the ability to be educated (in the best sense) and develop further through education. He can only endure what he already has inside himself; that he can acknowledge and develop. What he is taught from the outside, he rejects.

But if there should arise a teacher of mankind among us, we should already have developed all these abilities very well. Without the possibility to be able truly to receive the teachings, the appearance of a spiritual Master would be senseless.

Thus we would throw ourselves back into a spiritual loneliness.

Personal words

Every human being who is engaged in anthroposophy has different experiences with it – but also similar ones.

The very first experience that I had with the spiritual knowledge of Rudolf Steiner was the complete overcoming of the fear of death – through his rational knowledge of life after death (*Theosophy*). That is not knowledge like other knowledge. It is the gaining of an incomparable security in life. Only true knowledge can bring about such a transformation in one's feelings about life, so that the central fear relaxes, leading to the release of an incredible energy.

The second experience relates to the already present desire for self-education. The fact described by Rudolf Steiner, that the acquisition of spiritual knowledge is proportional to the soul's level of purification guaranteed for me the truth of this striving for the spirit. Continuous work on one's own capacity for compassion and love lies before the spiritual student alongside a permanent development of the capacity for knowledge itself: the development of the category of knowledge, of concentration, thinking exercises, living and judging in conformity with reality, self-observation (not during daily life, but in quiet moments), a continuously growing love for work, the growing feeling that the whole of life is an altar, on which one sacrifices one's gifts… Not that it always succeeds – it is a matter of always 'striving and trying hard'.

The third experience is the energy and joy of life which evolve out of the former two experiences.
Rudolf Steiner quoted Nietzsche once, who wrote about

Schopenhauer:[87]

'I belong to the readers of Schopenhauer, who after they have read the first pages of him, know with certainty, that they shall read all the pages and shall hear every word he said. I had faith in him at once... I understood him, as if he had written for me: in order to express myself understandably, but immodestly and foolishly.'

Rudolf Steiner felt the same about Nietzsche's work. I can say the same words again about Rudolf Steiner. Now, after 24 years of 'living together'[88] with the legacy of Rudolf Steiner and following his encouragement intensively, I still have not had enough of it in the slightest; every line still captivates me. I have still not found a single remaining contradiction – though periodically, there appeared to be some, of course – all of which daily still proves his work to be unshakeable truth, because everything can be followed up, not only as knowledge, but above all in the realization of the levels of knowledge described, which also leads to the real, living Rudolf Steiner.

Daily I still find new things in his work, also in books that I have worked through several times already. If I 'only read', I always have a slight feeling of guilt, because it must be much more intensive, the content of everything must be meditated, deepened, expanded. The Collected Works ('Gesamtausgabe') live, if the reader can (wants) to live in them, because they grow, becomes more and more, greater, more valuable. Never does the feeling arise: yes, yes, I know that already … on the contrary the feeling always remains: I can not completely appreciate it, although I can under-

---

[87] Rudolf Steiner, *Friedrich Nietzsche, A Fighter Against His Time*, GA 5, p.15

[88] Written in 2008

stand it very well. It reaches deeper, higher, further than I can experience. From this grows this burgeoning desire to ‚keep striving and trying hard'. While studying, I am not paralysed by boredom, but increasingly fascinated, for it leads into life - life in its different meanings: the life of one's biography and life of the etheric body, life in contradiction with death.

This Master teaches the ability to enable knowledge to become fact. And with that, beneath his whole work he places the signature of union with the divine being that enables heaven on earth to become a fact for us.

Written in consciousness of the imperfection of this presentation and with the deepest gratitude and respect for this Master of the Occident.

Baarle-Nassau, Easter Monday 2008
Mieke Mosmuller.

*

With gratefullness to the late Gabriele Savier-Dietz.

231

Literature

Erika Beltke/Kurt Viertl, *Erinnerungen an Rudolf Steiner*
(Memories of Rudolf Steiner), Stuttgart 2001
Andrej Belyj, *Mijn Jaren met Rudolf Steiner* (My Years With
Rudolf Steiner), Zeist 1989
Sergei O. Prokofieff, Rudolf Steiner and the Founding of the
New Mysteries, Temple Lodge, 1994
Friedrich Rittelmeyer, *Meine Lebensbegegnung mit Rudolf
Steiner* (My Life's Encounter with Rudolf Steiner), Stuttgart
1983
Albert Steffen, *Begegnungen mit Rudolf Steiner* (Meetings
with Rudolf Steiner), Dornach 1975
G. Wachsmuth, *Rudolf Steiners Erdenleben und Wirken*
(Rudolf Steiner's Earthly Life and Deeds), Dornach 1951
F. W. Zeylmans van Emmichhoven, Rudolf Steiner, *Rudolf
Steiner*, Stuttgart 1961
Rudolf Steiner, *Gesamtausgabe* (Collected Works), Dornach